Advance Praise for
Awakening Healing Axis

"This was a wonderful first experience at an AHA Retreat. Thank you for creating a beautiful, safe, and sacred space for us Light Beings to gather, learn, commune, and grow. I am full of gratitude. I am leaving fully connected deeper with my Soul and Core Essence, loving myself and the Divinity within me." –Dena A.

"This took my own healing to the next level. I feel much more a part of the earth's light matrix now. The activities on boundaries gave me a new understanding and awareness of others and my own choice of size of energy fields. The deep reminder of being my Core Essence transformed me from a reactive or low vibration state, I really am transformed! I have never experienced anything like these protocol exchanges and am deeply transformed and grateful. I will be using these protocols with clients. Thank you so much for upgrading my energy practice. I needed the self-love piece, thank you!" –Amy T. H.

"Wow! Quantum Hara Upgrade! So amazing of what a difference it made to my whole Being and how it strengthened and heightened the work and understanding of it!" –Penny M. H.

"The facilitators have a great ability to explain difficult concepts! The healing protocols felt easier to follow and understand compared to last year. Thank you for being awesome!" –Sylvie C.

"It was a fascinating experience for me personally. Much needed self-care. Eye opening!" –Nancy S.

"Explaining, demonstrating, and experiencing was a great sequence for the material presented. Discovering my Soul's purpose was the most exciting, affirming, and meaningful experience I have had in a very long time. Thank you!" –Jean P.

Amplifying
HIGHER FREQUENCIES

Awakening
Healing
Axis

A Guidebook to Embodying and Unearthing
Your Soul's Deeper Purpose

Awakening Healing Axis Presents
Co-Authors Franny Harcey & Tim McConville

Amplifying Higher Frequencies
A Guidebook to Embodying and Unearthing Your Soul's Deeper Purpose

This publication is published and distributed worldwide in the English language in the following formats:

ISBN Paperback: 978-1-953445-84-1
ISBN E-Book: 978-1-953445-85-8
Library of Congress Control Number: 2025940298

This book was printed in a manner that minimizes its impact on the planet and the environment. Learn more at:
www.inspirebytes.com/why-we-publish-differently/

 INSPIREBYTES OMNI MEDIA

Inspirebytes Omni Media LLC
PO Box 988
Wilmette, IL 60091
For more information, please visit www.inspirebytes.com.

AHA Statement

"Our mission is to raise the collective frequency of ourselves and those we support, so that we can aid in the ascension of human consciousness aligned with the highest Rays of Divine Love."

.

Table of Contents

Part 1

Fundamental Principles

Chapter One

Introduction

This fourth book is part of a continually expanding series that brings forth higher frequency work. As such, it builds on the foundation provided by the first three books in the series which are:

- *Awakening to Higher Frequencies*
- *Embodying Higher Frequencies: Accelerating Personal and Planetary Consciousness*
- *Revealing Higher Frequencies: A Guidebook to Exploring Personal Growth and Self-Love Through Deep Reflection Using the Divinity Mirror and Energetic Expressions*

These first books covered our work from 2020, 2021, and 2022. The work presented in this book represents Awakening Healing Axis' (AHA) thoughts following our Spring 2023 workshop/retreat, tenth in our ever-evolving body of work. Each workshop has focused on new topics and contained mostly new material. This specific workshop's primary focus was on the embodiment of our spiritual self. We also focused on self-love and self-compassion and finding the joy and awe in our lives. We pushed deeper into understanding our energetic selves and new ways to work with the body's fascia system. Spirit continues to nudge us to disseminate this work of raising our energetic frequency with more 1-day workshops and in print form with associated web-based visual teachings.

For those who have read the previous volumes, much of the background material will seem familiar. We continually make some changes as our understanding and perception shifts, so we recommend reviewing these sections, even if you have read our material previously. The guidebook portion describing experiential protocols for self and clients is mostly new material for your exploration.

Our early work was developed with the original triad of healers. As this work unfolds, we are urged to expand our contributors and facilitators. This volume includes work developed by our emerging team of associates.

In our 3rd book, we focused on self-development and understanding how the mirrors and filters of our beliefs and energetic coping mechanisms distort our worldview and interactions with others. We begin with focusing on self-love, as it seems to be at the root of our interactions with the world. We believe that we are here in "earth school" to learn lessons. All those lessons have something to do with love. Our ability to understand love is constrained by our ability to self-love. We also focused deeper into personal energetic boundaries and how we regulate those boundaries to interact with the energies of those around us. This self-discovery is a key aspect of learning to be more present and hold higher frequencies.

In order for humanity as a whole to awaken, we must each awaken as individuals. We are all connected on this planet, so our individual awakening contributes to the collective awakening. We are in a distinct time period for all of humanity to awaken and embrace our rapid evolution into a new energetic world. Rather than wait for the collective awakening to sweep us along, we invite you to be explorers at the forefront of this wave. This work provides essential tools for the self-transformation needed to sustain the energetic expressions of this evolutionary step. When we take those steps to move ourselves to a higher frequency, we can then become the conduit for healing the planet and lifting all others.

We are often asked what difference it makes if we raise our frequency or vibration. Let us start with clearing up a little language about vibration.

The New Age movement commonly uses the phrase "raising vibration." However, vibration is movement, and frequency is the rate of that movement. We are actually always vibrating, so we do not really "raise" the vibration. We raise the frequency or rate of the vibration.

Compare it to sound. Increasing vibration (volume) just makes things louder. Raising the frequency (pitch) of sound, however, moves it to a higher note. So we need to focus on frequency and move our energy to a higher note.

If we think about frequency within the context of our emotions and thoughts, lower frequencies are associated with more difficult and less joyful states such as anger, frustration, fear, and negativity. Higher frequency emotions are associated with more positive expressions such as love, joy, hope, and awe.

Spiritually, we are designed to constantly strive for closer connections to the Divine and experience deeper love. This too requires a higher frequency. Therefore, raising your frequency allows for greater happiness and more cohesive interpersonal relationships.

Additionally, many illnesses have psychosomatic components that have been linked to stress and long-term existence in states of lower frequency. This has been particularly noticeable in the realms of autoimmune disorders. Raising our frequency helps move us into a place of less disease and more efficient bodily function. The benefits of holding a higher frequency show up in a multitude of forms throughout our lives such as: improved health, deeper alignment with goals, more positive relationships, more stable and uplifted mental health, and a richer spiritual life.

We think it is important to have a daily practice of intentionally raising our frequency. Additionally, being mindful of frequency as we interact with others and the world throughout our day is also essential. Most of us cannot hold these higher frequencies without making a conscious effort to nudge it back up as it drifts down.

Higher frequency work is continuing to change those of us who facilitate Awakening Healing Axis in subtle ways. As we are better able to sustain higher frequency, it changes the way we work with clients, teach energy work classes, and interact with people in our lives. We have noticed that although we teach the exact same curriculum as our old classes, the students seem to be getting more out of them, and the work runs deeper. The collective continues to grow as we continue to facilitate, and those who have shared in workshops expand in awareness and are clearly all connected in this work. Spiritually, we sense that we are able to connect at a deeper level and receive greater guidance as our world has become much richer and more expansive. We are still quite capable of experiencing a lower frequency, but we find that we spend less time there and can pull ourselves up more easily.

Though easy to learn, the capacity to shift frequency requires continued practice. It has the potential to change each of us in amazing ways, and the ripples can change our entire planet. We believe frequency shift is one of the keys to human and planetary evolution.

Importance of Science

We strive to respect what we know in terms of current science, especially when we expand beyond the known limitations of our current understanding. Tim is trained in scientific methods and is keenly interested in the scientific understanding of our wonderful world. When referring to scientific principles, we do our best to be accurate within our understanding.

It is also important to realize the nature of scientific study. As a society, we are continually learning new things about our world. If we stop to think about it, we realize that almost all science texts from our college days are virtually useless due to the expansion in knowledge. One generation from now, scientific understanding will have again exponentially increased. How can we possibly state that we completely understand our world when every day there is a new scientific discovery in areas we thought we understood?

We need to respect scientific understandings yet not let them limit us from exploring beyond those confines. Any good physicist will agree that there are many more dimensions than the 3D view suggests. Various theories predict from 11 to 30 dimensions or more, yet we know almost nothing about these spaces. As such, it is important for us to both include science in the conversation and remain open to its ever-evolving nature and our understanding of the world.

How to Use This Work

This work is laid out as a guidebook. That means we will describe how we work and our perspective on the energetic world. Additionally, we offer you guided protocols to use these concepts. The protocols can be used on oneself to aid in healing and personal transformation. They can also be used by an experienced energy therapist to work with clients. We consider this to be advanced work that adds to the skillset of practitioners trained in one or more healing modalities.

When we facilitate this work in workshops, we find the work is repeatable. Our theory is that in the workshop setting, the facilitators model the energetic frequency of the guides and the work. Through the entrainment process, the energy systems of the participant resonate with the frequencies of the facilitator(s). The participant is then able to reproduce those frequencies once exposed. It does not require conscious awareness or understanding on the part of the participant. Their energy system does what is required on a subconscious level.

Of course, we realize that not everybody will have the time, money, and flexibility required to physically attend one of our workshops in person. Although not as powerful as a full immersion experience like the workshop, written, audio, and web-based visual participation will still transfer a good portion of the subtle frequencies that define the depth of this work. We have found that recorded audios and video serve a respectable role in transmitting and entraining these frequencies.

It is our sincere hope that the combination of printed material and web-based video content will provide the proper combination of material that satisfies both the mind's need for information and the heart's need for energetic connections. We have seen immense transformations in our workshop participants. Our hope is that broader availability of the material can aid many more people in their healing and make a positive impact on humanity.

Chapter Two

Importance of
Higher Frequencies

As energy therapy and healing practitioners, we are often confronted with situations of chaos and fear. Some are more extreme than others, but nevertheless they all tug at our own insecurities and may trigger trauma and/or unresolved personal issues. The question then becomes: "How do we stay afloat in these stormy seas of energies and provide a safe refuge for ourselves and others?" On the surface, it would seem as if our daily self-care, peaceful life choices, and healing work are enough to fend off the destructive forces of judgment, prejudice, hatred, fear, shame, guilt, or arrogance. This is not an easy nor simple task, especially when we are confronted by unexpected and/or extreme situations.

The ability to shift our frequency is something everyone can learn, but it requires continued practice and attention. Personal commitment to this choice can shift each of us in amazing ways. One of the first tools for manifesting such a shift is discernment. There are many "channels" of energy—or energetic radio stations—in the energy realms. We are bombarded in our daily interactions with numerous aspects of the lower frequency channels, many of which are reinforced by social media, marketing, and many of the news headlines. The much more desirable higher frequency channels, such as "selfless love" and "random acts of kindness," are not publicized as often nor made popular by the media. Thus, it becomes very important to proactively tune in to the bigger picture of what is really happening. Good discernment involves asking if this situation or information is of the Light, and whether it should be accepted or ignored. One of the easiest ways to be proactive in our discernment is to tune in to nature.

In the natural world, spring is a time of new energies and perhaps the easiest time to see new beauty in nature. However, no matter what the season, we can always be nourished by what nature offers to help keep us grounded and whole. Choosing to tune in to nature and a more positive worldview changes our overall perceptions and raises our frequency. Take the time to drink in the mystery of nature's beauty and the inherent goodness of humanity. Awe and wonder can shift our body, emotions, mind, and Spirit to states of bliss and joy, giving us a glimpse of the altered states of the mystics and prophets. Choose compassion and take the "high road" as much as possible.

Unfortunately, mass media seems to choose the extremes, demonizing or falsely elevating people. Everyone is a mix of both good and bad. No one is without flaws. All we can hope for is to act like our better selves most of the time. We are all in this together, and the more we support one another and work as a synergistic team, the more we will be able to fuel hope and help maintain our individual and collective equilibrium. In this manner, each of us can hold space for the ongoing evolution and ascension of humanity and our planet.

In our collective work, we focus on strengthening and broadening the deepest cores of our human and spiritual existence. This involves high frequency techniques and protocols for transmuting and elevating our abilities to be fully present in this realm, all the while anchored into the core of our earth. This empowers us to stand as conduits for Divine energies of unconditional love. Furthermore, by fully embodying our Divine light as human and Spirit, we have the ability to step into a space of healing at a quantum level. From this place, we can help raise the frequency of our clients and others around us to support the healing and enlightenment of all.

Chapter Three

How We Work

Our original triad was drawn together in the process of various activities in the Healing Touch Program (HTP) organization. The founder of the Healing Touch Program, Janet Mentgen, also serves as a Guide to our work as Awakening Healing Axis (AHA). When instructing previous HTP classes, we often felt Janet's presence in the classroom although Janet had left the earth plane. We also sense her presence and guidance in this more advanced work. As presenters and active members in national and international-level organizational activities, we would frequently connect with each other and compare notes about our expanding energetic interests. We found that we were each getting nudged by Spirit to expand the work beyond the envelope of current HTP teachings.

Sometime around 2016, we decided to work together to create an advanced workshop. As the planning unfolded, we realized that this was bigger than one workshop. Led by Spirit, we all said "Yes!" and we committed to the unknown by formalizing a business partnership to move the work forward. We have found the idea of working as a triad to be quite valuable. Discernment is critical in guided or channeled work. The triad organizational model provided the necessary validation checks for each other and allowed expanded creativity. Often one of us gets a part of the information, and the others build on it and expand to find what was missing. The old saying "two minds are better than one" seems enhanced by adding a third. Though the original triad has changed by one stepping away, we maintain the energy of a triad because a new person moved into that position.

We continue to work in triads or larger groups as we believe it is important to get clarification and validation of guided input. Input from the guides can come in the quiet times of meditation for any of the group or perhaps as we ponder the work, or when writing. Often when we are collaborating with clients, we get guidance to shift the energy in new and unusual ways. During our times together, we may collectively hone the work brought in by one of us, or we may bring in innovative ideas on potential energetic topics. All the creative ideas and techniques are tested with willing clients and refined prior to bringing the healing work forward in a workshop. Often, information comes in swiftly and takes time to unpack and re-package in a suitable workshop format. A 20-minute burst of the latest information can take months to translate into teachable workshop segments. Part of that translation process is to find appropriate real-world analogs that can help bridge the understanding.

We believe that it is important that this more esoteric work weaves with current scientific understanding of our world and the physical body where possible. This allows us to understand how energetic work complements medical interventions within the limitations of ever-expanding scientific knowledge.

Chapter Four

Energetic Framework

To really access the work in this book, it is important to first understand our viewpoint of the unseen aspects of the human energetic system. This understanding both informs the work and assists in directing the intent of our protocols.

We believe our existence on this planet is far more complex than the physical and mental framework often portrayed by scientific understanding. Our existence and interactions with others is a multidimensional experience. The understanding we offer builds upon the teachings of other mystics and explorers of this area. Over time, our guides have continued to expand our understanding of this framework. If you have studied this subject widely enough, you are aware that there are inconsistencies in terminology and differing explanations.

We liken this phenomenon to the old story of a group of blind men describing an elephant as they touch distinct parts. Each may be correct yet provide only a partial view of the whole.

Just like the blind men in the story, we are limited in the ways we experience the world beyond our five senses. Each of us—each energetic explorer—has different gifts to experience the unseen. All may be correct, but all are still limited by the gifts of the seer. So what happens when we are faced with the significant issue of our human desire to linearize and fit the multidimensional universe into a 3D box? It simply does not work. It would be akin to making two-dimensional drawings of ten-dimensional objects just so they fit in a book.

Therefore, the following is our attempt to describe our current and ever-evolving understanding of our energetic framework. In offering this information, we acknowledge that our limited human minds are only marginally capable of accurately understanding and translating the infinite into the finite. Again, like the blind men, we can report what we see with accuracy, but the true scope of the whole still resides in the mist.

We think of ourselves in this human existence as a bridge between heaven and earth. We are very much a Spirit and part of all that exists in the realm of Spirit, while our lessons are solidly placed in this school on the planet earth. Our description of our energetic framework begins with the earth that we are connected to, then moves back to our origin, which is in the realm of Spirit, in order to describe how we transcend both of these realms.

Grounding

Being grounded in this earthly existence is probably one of the most important—yet least practiced—spiritual disciplines. Although there are many techniques and plenty of teachers with this message, there seem to be few people who can consistently put it into practice. The combination of 1) a western culture that overvalues the mental, and 2) spiritual guidance that shames the physical and directs our gaze upward has created a culture of people living in the upper Chakras.

We passionately believe that we are all at the juncture of heaven and earth. We have a choice to be that bridge between the two, or the gap between the two. For many workshop participants, it seems counterintuitive that to raise our frequency high, we must first connect deeply below. We have seen many times when working with workshop participants that the key to accessing the energy of above is to first look below. We suggest that an important part of any healing work discipline is to start with the awareness of being grounded and consciously connected to the earth.

The hard part is to then maintain that connection and stay grounded while experiencing lofty higher frequencies and multiple dimensions. One of the keys to achieving this is practice. With practice, we can spread the awareness of being grounded and in the present moment to our everyday life. We aren't suggesting that it is likely we will stay grounded at every waking moment, but slowly gaining a larger percentage of our day would be an achievable goal.

While being grounded is important in spiritual work, it does have benefits in our everyday activities. When we are grounded, we tend to be more aware of our surroundings. We are more able to see the beauty of nature and the people around us. When grounded, we are also less scattered and more present. Our personal interactions and conversations are far richer when we are grounded and paying attention to others. A great many of those moments of forgetfulness or absent-minded mistakes come from being ungrounded. When we forget where we misplaced something, it's probably because we put it down while our mind was in the past or future and we were ungrounded. Grounding is an aspect of being present—of living in the now.

Pure Timeless Earth Template

As noted above, we are big proponents of connecting or "grounding" to the earth. In our practice, we have noticed that many people, especially the more sensitive people, have trouble connecting to our planet. Some people more naturally "ground" into other elements than earth. Some prefer water, air, wood, ether, or some other substances. Many sensitive people find the earth feels unsafe to them, which makes it difficult to ground into the earth—or stay grounded if they are able to connect to it. We have been striving to find a way for these people to feel safe enough to make a deeper connection to the planet, which we share in more detail below through the concept of Gaia.

Another phenomenon that is occurring is the ascension movement. Numerous groups and individuals around the planet are participating in efforts to shift the energetic frequency of the planet, moving earth and its inhabitants into a higher frequency or dimension. Most of these efforts are good; however, there is some distortion. It seems to us that although the effort is good, there is a lack of cohesion, and divergent groups have slightly different ideas about the frequency and direction in which we are headed. We liken the situation to an orchestra warming up with instruments out of tune. We are lacking a common note to harmonize with, that would allow us to come into perfect cohesion.

Our suggested solution to these issues is termed "Pure Timeless Earth Template." Rather than tuning into the current earth, or the idea of an evolving earth, we offer the idea of a Divine template of a pure projection of perfect earth in resonance with the organizing principles of the universe. Another way to think of this is to use the idea of Gaia. This idea has the earth as a manifestation of a Divine being. If we think of connecting with the pure essence of Gaia, we will ground into the pure, Divine aspects of the earth. When offered a model of connecting to the Divine aspect of the earth—or the Pure Timeless Earth—most people can more readily ground and feel safer connecting to the frequency of earth. The Pure Timeless Earth offers a consistent, safe frequency that all of us can use to come into harmony and resonance.

We have adopted the Pure Timeless Earth Template in all of our grounding exercises. Our Hara, grounding, and Vivaxis connecting exercises all now use this frequency to hold connection to our planet. We have found that this provides a stronger and more pure connection. We are noticing a deeper degree of connection to the planet, the ability to hold the connection longer, and greater ease of coming into resonance with the matrix of the earth. Many who were once hesitant to energetically connect with our earth can now embrace her at this new frequency.

We will refer to the Pure Timeless Earth Template as Pure Timeless Earth for simplicity.

Core Essence

We think of Core Essence as our true self—the fundamental, multidimensional, spiritual being that we are. This is the purest aspect of who we are and is in resonance with the oneness of everything. At this level, we are pure and untainted by the trials and tribulations of living on earth. This aspect of our being is not harmed and never traumatized. Core Essence exists in a different dimension. This highest frequency of our spiritual being cannot be fully experienced on the physical plane. Just as electricity is stepped down from high voltage lines by transformers to household current levels, our Core Essence gets stepped down into the lower frequencies of our existence to manifest on the physical plane.

We consider soul to be a subset of Core Essence. Soul holds more earthbound characteristics. Perhaps soul is more like the level of consciousness needed to bridge the dimensional realities and manage our lessons while on the earth plane. Our concept of Core Essence is like what Barbara Brennan described in her book, *Light Emerging*, as Core Star.[1] Her visuals of Core Star show it as located in the middle of the body, just above the navel. That may have been generally true in 1993 when her work was published, but we now visualize that it normally expresses itself at a higher location in the body and is more adaptable to movement. Core Essence exists in another dimension, so it is not actually present in the physical body as tissue. Visually identifying these aspects within our physical self is a useful tool that helps our limited minds work with these concepts.

Keep in mind that Core Essence is a higher dimension of self and not really located within the physical realm, yet it can be perceived to be located somewhere along the centerline of the body. As we mature spiritually, it can be perceived as moving higher in the physical body. In fact, humanity's collective evolution is allowing Core Essence to move higher and higher. Our concept of Core Essence allows greater fluidity and movement with an individual's frequency. Our work encourages that elevation with the goal of raising the perceived location out of the space of physical manifestation and into the spiritual energetic layers.

We sense Core Essence to be quite a malleable part of our energy self. It can be expanded, contracted, and elevated as one learns to master and better regulate the expression of their energetic being.

The Hara

Our understanding of the Hara is rooted in the work of Barbara Brennan. We believe that channeled work from the 1990s is a solid foundation. However, we are constantly evolving in an energetic sense. Therefore, it is best to see the earlier work as a good introduction, realizing that we may now be different in subtle and important ways. The Hara exists in the dimension of intention. Decades ago,

---

1 Brennan, B. A. (1993). *Light Emerging; The Journey of Personal Healing.* Bantam Books.

Brennan's work suggested that it was the fourth dimension. Our guidance now tells us to simply say another dimension rather than labeling any specific dimension.

Defining the Hara requires an understanding of the concept that our intent to incarnate on planet earth manifests an energetic connection

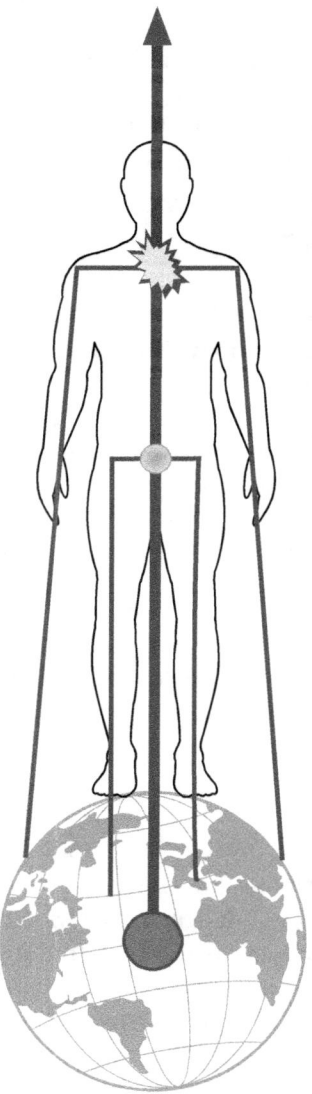

between our Core Essence and the earth. That energetic connection is held in place by the intentionality of being incarnate and becomes the basis and foundation for our physical and energetic bodies. Although the Hara is probably a multidimensional holographic projection, Brennan's description is much easier to understand.

The Hara begins to take form with the intent to incarnate, which means it begins to manifest well before our birth. In our work, we have sensed an incoming child's energy system well before conception. The Hara, therefore, is a line of energy connected to the core of planet earth. Along that line of energy there are three aspects of the Hara: the Tan Tien, the Soul Seat, and the Point of Individuation (ID). The Tan Tien is in our lower abdomen. The Soul Seat is near the thymus gland, and the ID point is located at a point above our head where the aura starts. This book introduces four additional Hara aspects, which will be described in a later section. Keep in mind that the Hara is in another dimension, so it will not be physically found within the body.

The Hara becomes the foundation of our earthly energetic system. Brennan also describes the Hara as carrying a unique, specific sound note or frequency. That unique individual frequency is part of the definition of who we are on this planet. Our Chakras and fields then develop around the Hara. Each of the three aspects of the Hara have certain characteristics:

- The Tan Tien carries the note and makes the physical connection to the Hara. The Tan Tien is used extensively in martial arts training.
- The Soul Seat holds our spiritual longings and desires.
- The ID point holds our connection to Spirit or Divine energy.

As the Hara holds our intentionality to be on earth, it also contains a connection to our life's purpose. The stronger and more aligned one's Hara is, the better the realization and alignment to life's purpose. Subsequently, if one's intentionality to be on earth is not clear, it will energetically appear as some level of distortion in the Hara.

Brennan described the Hara as a laser line of light, and students carry forward that visual of a very thin Hara line. However, it is our experience that the Hara can be much wider. Perhaps it is due to evolutionary shifts in our energy structure over the last few decades. Our perspective is that a wider Hara can carry more energy. We often use the metaphor of a garden hose versus a fire hose. The larger hose allows for a much greater flow of water, so a larger Hara allows more energy flow. That said, we also caution that one needs to be able to regulate and control the amount of energy flow. Bigger is not necessarily better if you cannot properly use it.

We have been slowly increasing the size and expansion of the Hara that we teach in our work. One must slowly increase the size as they learn to regulate and control the extra energy. At a recent workshop, we had participants expand and experience an increasingly wider Hara with instructions to bring it back to what felt right after experiencing the expansion. There were several reports of people then having tripped circuits and experiencing other electrical issues with the technological devices in their lives. One even reported seeing a light that would not go out, unscrewing the bulb, and having the bulb still glowing in their hand. Although amusing, such dysregulation is not very

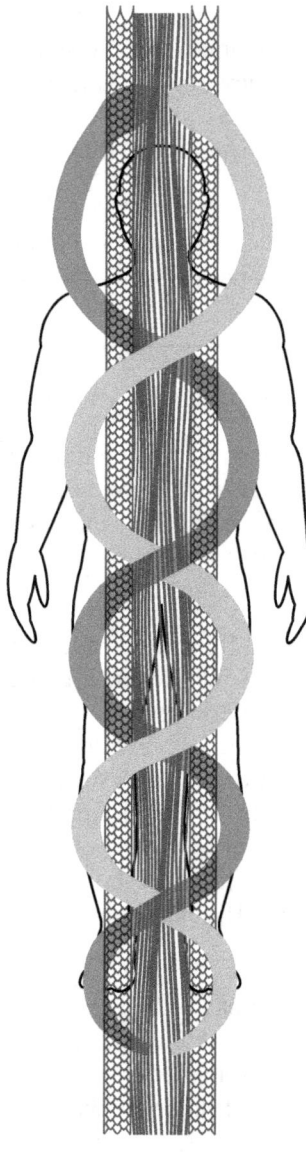

practical for living in our normal 3D realities. We need to effectively manage these new, higher frequencies of being.

We also experience and bring forward the visualization that the Hara has four strengthening lines that are not separate from the Hara, but part of it. They connect to the existing three aspects we have already discussed. From the Tan Tien, lines extend to each hip and down each leg. From the Soul Seat, lines extend to each shoulder and down each arm. These pillars (as the previous graphic depicts) support additional grounding into the gridlines and matrices of the Pure Timeless Earth, inviting stronger connection to our planet.

The Hara has structure, both internal and external. We sense the outside structure of the Hara as a woven expression with the weave spiraling in both clockwise and counterclockwise directions. Similarly, there seem to be internal structures of opposite spirals, much the way Kundalini energy is often depicted.

The Hara can distort in a wide variety of ways. Distortion can be related to past life trauma or lack of clarity in the intentionality of incarnation. Traumas in this life can also impact the Hara, causing leaks, tears, or distortions. Distortions may cause it to tilt at an angle either above or below, limiting connections to either earth or Source energies. A healthy Hara should be straight, like a column of light. Leaks and tears in the Hara may limit access to full energy flow and ultimately can lead to disease or illness. The Hara can also become weak and poorly defined when intent to be on earth wanes. We have seen this at the end of life or even in children who are struggling with life on earth, having recently reincarnated.

The Hara, like all aspects of our energy structure, can be healed, upgraded, and repaired with the help of skilled energy workers. These helpers could be incarnate or in the spirit realm. Our work includes practices to repair and keep regular energetic hygiene of our Hara and also helps our clients do the same.

The Vivaxis

The Vivaxis and the Hara are completely different energetic structures and likely exist in different dimensions. Both are equally important but in quite diverse ways. The Hara begins sometime before conception or during our time in the womb, whereas the Vivaxis energetically makes a connection near the time of our birth. We choose to incarnate into a specific family in a certain physical location for our lessons in earth school. The Vivaxis is a specific connection to the earth that you anchor into at that location on the earth where you choose to incarnate.

We create a little energetic sphere that anchors in and to the earth and connects to us as we move around, like a virtual cord. It stays anchored there throughout your lifetime unless it is intentionally moved to a different location. This cord allows energy to flow, completing a circuit between the earth and ourselves. Our bones and fascia are the chief carriers of our Vivaxis forces. The Vivaxis is an anchoring force to the earth. When clear and flowing, the Vivaxis feeds us with minerals and nutrients from the earth. This flow is on a frequency level and does not actually transport minerals physically.

We sense this flow of energy via the Vivaxis coming into the body up the left leg. We sense it quite strongly, almost like a hose in the lower leg and bones. As it moves up the leg, it begins to disperse into the fascia tissues as well. It continues up the body, crossing the heart to the right side, then moves up around the head from right to left. It then flows back down, crossing the heart again, and exits the body along the entire right side. We find it more difficult to sense the return flow on the right as it is much more dispersed than the concentrated flow coming into the body.

We have also become aware that the Vivaxis is somehow energetically interwoven with the 10th Chakra. We do not sense that the Vivaxis flow is through the 10th Chakra; however, it seems that changes in the Vivaxis interact with and affect the 10th Chakra. That interaction could be in the quantum relationships of all aspects of our energy system.

The primary focus of our work is to help people reestablish and maintain healthy Vivaxis connections. Prior to joining together, we had dabbled with the concept of Vivaxis connections and were aware of the books on the subject. However, it was not until we were working together with AHA that we began to understand the importance of the Vivaxis. We recommend reading *The Vivaxis Connection* by Judy Jacka, ND, who had studied Fran Dixon's work. Again, we see this early work as a good foundation, although we have a somewhat different sense about certain aspects. Jacka goes into a great amount of detail about the chemical aspects of the Vivaxis, which we have not felt drawn to explore yet. We feel that this would be a great area of exploration for someone who focuses on energetic rather than product-based approaches to micronutrition.

Our healing work includes sensing and working with the Vivaxis. As healers, it is important that we do our self-care work and maintain a healthy Vivaxis. When assessing our own or a client's energy system, the Vivaxis is an important element to check. When working locally, we usually do this while standing at or holding the client's feet. When working remotely or for self, we just tune in to the flow of energy in the Vivaxis.

To do this, the first step is to feel into the Vivaxis flow at the left foot to assess the connection. Then focus on the energetic sphere where the Vivaxis connects to the earth. It is possible that the sphere is not functioning properly or is not integrated into the gridwork of the earth at that locality. Sometimes it appears the sphere is just dormant. When assessing and working with the sphere, again ask for help from Spirit. Visualize the sphere as radiant. Ask that the energetic structure of the sphere be upgraded and allow it to fuse and integrate with the highest frequencies of the local earth matrix.

For many people, the Vivaxis has just become sluggish and less effective, analogous to a pipe that has become clogged and corroded. For those cases, ask the spirit helpers to help shift the Vivaxis flow to its optimum function at this time. We often envision iridescent colors flowing into the Vivaxis as it is cleared and restructured.

Unfortunately, for some people, the Vivaxis does not even connect to the earth. We have seen a few individuals where the Vivaxis seems to float above the earth, not connecting to it, or even connecting to a portal or other dimensions. Sometimes trauma related to the original connection, or a distortion of the earth at the original connection, makes it difficult to reestablish a good connection. In some cases, it has been beneficial to move the Vivaxis connection to a more

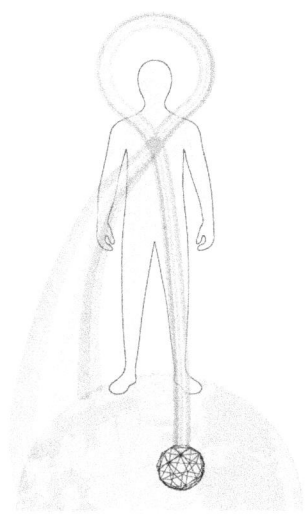

supportive location on earth. Moving the Vivaxis should not be taken lightly and should only be done with spiritual help and guidance. Additionally, moving it to a place based on ego-related whims may not be in the person's highest good. The work of Jacka and Dixon suggests that the movement of the Vivaxis needs to be done with a physical process. We believe it can be managed by the purest of intentions and projection of consciousness.

The Chakra System

The techniques and the energetic framework we are given include a considerable amount of work with the Chakra system. We initially focused primarily on the traditional seven Chakras, but also worked with some of the Chakras not contained in the body structure. There is a sizable amount of inconsistent information regarding Chakras in the world. A quick search of the internet yielded systems ranging from six to 114 different Chakras, and there are probably even more ideas out there. In general, our view of the Chakra system is similar to the 12-Chakra system described by author Cyndi Dale. We suggest referencing her material for a deeper explanation of the Chakras. Our explanations below will only provide enough information to locate the Chakras and work with them within the broader context of our higher frequency techniques.

Chakras are concentrated energy centers in and around our body. Chakras function as part of our sensory system and regulate energy flows to keep our body functioning at optimum levels. Although the term Chakra comes from the Sanskrit term for wheel or disk, we think the torus is a better explanation for the shape of a Chakra. The torus is a basic natural shape of energetic structures.

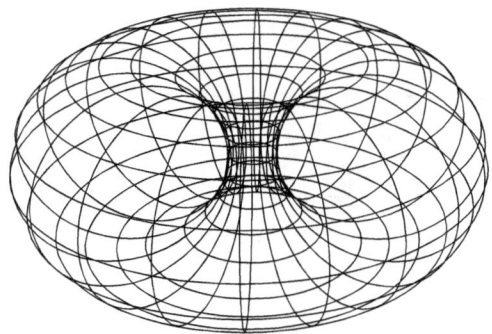

Examples of toroidal energy flow are exhibited throughout nature from the largest galactic structures to the tiniest biological functions and even smaller. This is the shape that concentrations of electromagnetic energy take. Viewing Chakras from this natural perspective also validates both of the common beliefs that Chakras look like both disks and cones, depending on the viewer's perspective.

We previously thought of the Chakras as having a front side, a back side, and a center point that connects front and back. That concept fits with the cone paradigm of Chakras; however, it does not fit the torus paradigm of Chakras. We are now reframing the front aspect as the conscious aspect, which is governed by the physical laws, relating to the conscious self and our day-to-day realities. It holds and senses information about our current life, needs, decisions, and experiences. The conscious aspect allows the tangible world to help us.

The back aspect, previously labeled as "back," is now termed "unconscious." It is governed by limitless alternative realities, represents the unconscious self and information about our past. It holds imprints from our past lives, past experiences and decisions, and needs. The unconscious aspect allows the intangible world to help us.

The center point we sometimes refer to as the "zero point." The center point of the Chakra is located along the central channel of the energy system or Hara. The center point is the access point of pure potential or the zero point field. When the central point is activated, we can call in the next expression of our highest l.ght. The zero point can seem to be formless; we often experience it as opening into a vast, spiraling galaxy or universe.

The following is a brief description of each of the Chakras. As previously stated, there are many excellent books that describe aspects of the Chakras in depth, so we don't feel the need to repeat that information.

1st – Root: Located at pelvic floor; Iridescent red.
Conscious aspect: This is our basic, primal survival Chakra (tribal). It is instinctual and about our physical health and presence on the planet.
Unconscious aspect: Holds keys to our unconscious beliefs about deserving physical life and well-being, regulates the physical system and flow of universal energy.

2nd – Sacral: Located just below the navel; Iridescent orange.
Conscious aspect: The expression of feelings and creativeness with the world. Our connectivity to all others and our sexuality.
Unconscious aspect: Supports the unconscious template of the conscious aspect. Supports us through changes and adaptations.

3rd – Solar plexus: Located at solar plexus, just below the sternum; Iridescent yellow.
Conscious aspect: The source of our self-esteem and self-power, our ability to succeed in the world. Our thoughts and mental structures.
Unconscious aspect: Our mental templates of self and how the world works.

4th – Heart: Located at center of chest, near nipple line; Iridescent green.
Conscious aspect: Love and ability to give and receive with others. Heart balances the lower and upper Chakras.
Unconscious aspect: Connection to our heart's desire, unconscious belief about love and relationships with others and the Divine.

5th – Throat: Located at base of throat; Iridescent sky blue.
Conscious aspect: Expression, communication, and creativity. Alignment of will and guidance from Spirit.
Unconscious aspect: Access point for external spiritual guidance.

6th – Brow: Located at center of the forehead, just above the brow; Iridescent indigo.
Conscious aspect: Seat of the mind, dreaming, intuition, and wisdom. Connection to higher levels of compassion and connection of all humanity.
Unconscious aspect: Our potential and access to higher wisdom and vision.

7th – Crown: Located on top of the head; Iridescent violet.
Conscious aspect: Seat of the spirit and truth. How we project our spiritual beliefs and programming. Connection to "knowing."
Unconscious aspect: Opens us to the Divine, filtered by our belief systems.

8th – Gateway: Located several inches above the head; Iridescent silver.
Conscious aspect: Expression of your life purpose. Interacts with beings of different dimensions and planes of existence.
Unconscious aspect: Expression of karmic and past choices influencing what you attract to your life. Work through past and future lives and visit parallel or concurrent realities.

9th – Soul Star: Located 1–2 feet above the head; Iridescent copper.
Conscious aspect: Projection of your Soul's understanding of love. How you care for and connect with others.
Unconscious aspect: Your Soul's desires and beliefs about love and the world.

10th – Earth Star: Located several inches to a few feet into the earth below our feet; Iridescent earth tone.
Conscious aspect: Our interactions with the world and natural materials.
Unconscious aspect: Aspects of the natural world you connect with. Ancestral lineages that you bring forward. DNA and epigenetic activations, both positive and negative.

The 11th and 12th Chakras are more encompassing and holistic in nature, all flowing together.

11th – Connective: Iridescent metallic blue. Associated with the hands and feet as well as muscles and connective tissue. Our sense is that it is energetically intertwined with the fascial system. Fascia is electrically conductive and connected to every cell in our body. As such, it is part of the internet of the body.

12th – Golden Matrix: Iridescent gold. Connects all physical elements into the outer layers of the energetic shell that surrounds us.

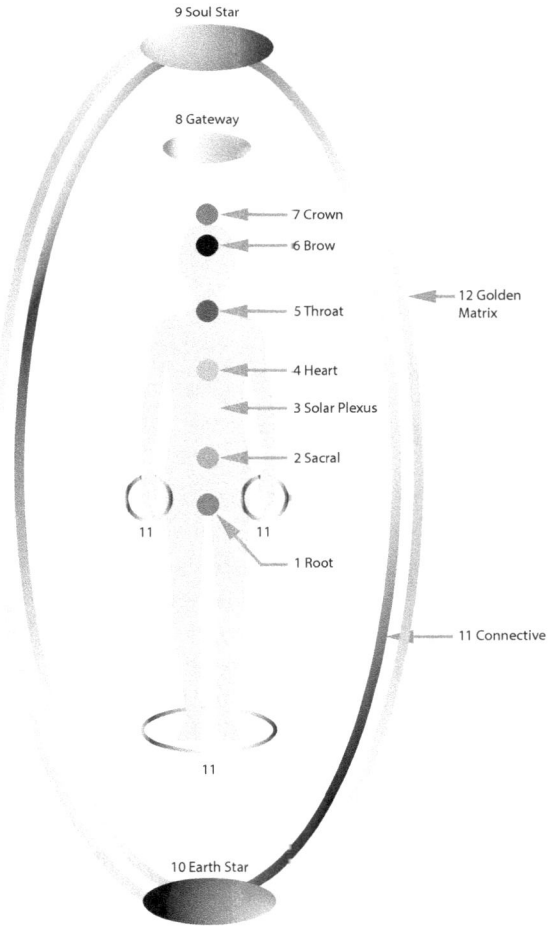

High Heart Portal

High Heart is located just above your Heart Chakra. We use the term "High Heart" for an energetic structure in the physical region of the thymus, closely interwoven with the Heart Chakra and Soul Seat aspect of Hara. We sense that the High Heart is not a Chakra, but rather an access point or a portal. The High Heart interacts with Heart Chakra and is involved in weaving information about your Soul purpose from the Hara through all the levels of your field, aligning with soul's purpose. Connecting with your High Heart Portal gives you access directly to your soul purpose and plans. You also have the ability and free will to change those plans.

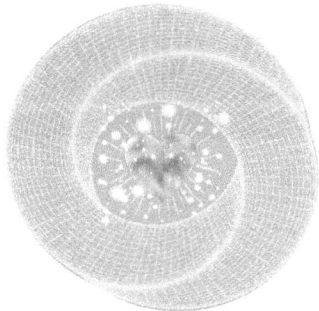

Chakra/Hara Unification

Our work is based on the idea that our Chakras have been experiencing an evolution. The current version of our work is based on the premise that we have already made this evolutionary step. This evolution of the Chakras has come as we clear old challenges and elevate into higher frequencies and Lightbody transformations. During this evolutionary step, the Chakra torus becomes expanded, allowing the frequencies and colors to blend and unify with the Hara. This may spontaneously happen if we have done the work to clear old patterns and shift our energetic being. Once unified, the Chakras function more in unison and communicate more clearly.

We have developed protocols to encourage and specifically invite in this transformation. This protocol is detailed in our book: *Awakening to Higher Frequencies: A Guidebook.*

Chakra Fusion

This portion of the work is based on another energetic evolution. As our frequency elevates, we reach a point where the lower seven Chakras blend and fuse. This allows them to work more effectively as a unit as our system relies more on the upper, more spiritually-related Chakras. Franny was given a vision of this Chakra Fusion back in 2013, and the concept lay dormant for five years until we received guidance that it should be incorporated into a 2019 workshop. The energy of this was in the collective, although it was only taught to a small group of people.

The fusing of the Chakras creates a blending of the Root Chakra with Crown Chakra, Sacral Chakra with Brow Chakra, Solar Plexus Chakra with Throat Chakra, and Heart Chakra with High Heart Portal. These four separate fusions allow the lower seven Chakras to create a strong vertical alignment of the toruses. We encourage you to include this evolution into your energetic system. We taught this protocol again in our spring 2024 workshop. It is available as an instructional module as part of the High Frequency Shift: Quantum Evolution in our online learning center and will be published in the next book in this series.

The Human Energy Field (HEF)

Our human energy field (HEF) is made of a series of torus-shaped fields that surround our entire physical body. Each field is associated with a Chakra. The figure, next page top, illustrates the first ten Chakras, each depicted as a spinning torus. Each torus creates a corresponding field surrounding the body. The fields are all axially centered along the central channel of the Hara. Each Chakra as we go up the numbers carries a higher frequency, which allows the field to extend further from the edge of the physical body. Some of these layers are composed of lines and grids (odd numbered fields: 1, 3, 5, 7, 9) and some are amorphous and more vapor-like (even numbered fields: 2, 4, 6, 8). The figure, next page bottom, illustrates the toruses plus the 11th and 12th fields. A picture showing all twelve fields is too difficult to show as they all blend together.

The common 7 Chakra/Field model that most people use is workable, and our experience tells us it is pretty accurate, but it's only a partial picture. An inquisitive mind might start asking questions about the other Chakras. If there are more than seven Chakras, why would only some create fields? Our sense is that our HEF is actually more complex than the simple model would explain.

Our experience suggests that the 8th field is amorphous with a white or pearlescent glow. The 9th field is firmer, creating a shell-like structure. The 10th field is both amorphous and firm. As the 10th radiates up, it joins with the 9th creating an overlay that envelopes the body in an egg-shaped bubble. We find the 11th a bit more complex as it seems to create its own layer yet is interwoven as a web connecting everything in the fields. The 12th is again more firm, creating a golden bubble as the edge of our field structure.

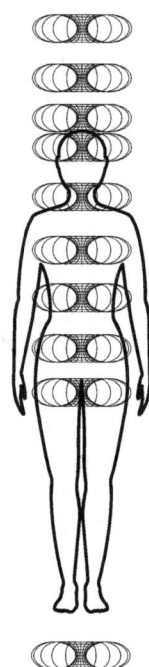

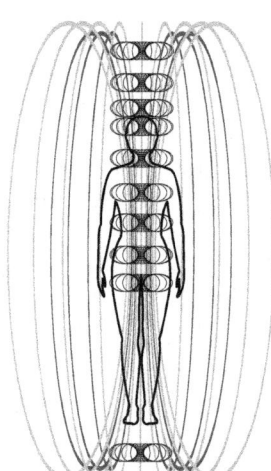

We don't think the field structure ends with the Chakra-related fields. Once we start looking at how we interact with the multidimensional universe, our Soul, and group consciousness, things get more complicated. Our total energy body or Lightbody holds information and coding in additional fields and grids. In the next section, we will attempt to explain some of these additional fields or grids that are currently in our awareness.

Additional Components of the HEF

We preface this section with the disclaimer that we know our understanding is inherently incomplete and approximate. These additional components of the HEF operate multidimensionally and quantumly. Thus most people, and certainly we, have a difficult time making sense of it.

The problem is that our mental models of the world are built in the three dimensions of space (length, width, and depth) plus the fourth dimension of time. However, physics theories require additional dimensions for mathematical consistency in explaining our world. Various physics theories require either 10, 11, 26, or 33 dimensions for all the math to work.

Our brains are not particularly good at conceptualizing things in 10 dimensions, and things really start falling apart as we attempt to visualize in 33 dimensions. Many times, we have come up with models or explanations that we thought captured the ideas we were working with; however, when we run it by our guides for verification, we get an answer such as: "Well it is closer, but still not right," or more commonly: "You are trying to linearize the nonlinear—it is more complicated."

So we invite you to read what we have to offer as a glimpse into a multidimensional quantum world that is fascinating beyond our ability to comprehend. We sometimes get confused about whether something is a grid (more structured) or field (more amorphous), as some of these layers seem to be both or seem to shift between the two. In the end, however, perhaps it is not so important which one they are, as it is more important to acknowledge their existence. These additional components of the HEF include:

- The Grand Matrix
- The Incarnation Grid
- The Soul Field
- The Fascial Grid
- Other Organizing Fields and Grids
- The Primary Cell

The Grand Matrix

When using the term "The Matrix," many are drawn to notions influenced by the 1999 science fiction movie of that title. However, the concepts of the Matrix presented by the movie have only partial relationships to what we view as reality.

In our thinking, the Matrix is a vast, fractal-like web structure that creates and organizes the universe or multiverse. What we think of as the "Grand Matrix" is the organizing consciousness of the Creator that pervades everything in all dimensions. We think of this matrix as carrying the instructions and organizing frequencies needed for every level of creation.

Within the Grand Matrix, there are many submatrices for each level of organization. The galaxy, the solar system, the planet, and each living creature have their own matrix, all of which interact with and are part of the Grand Matrix. The structure of our individual matrix contains the organizing principles, frequencies, and code to maintain our physical and energetic systems and guides us on our journey in this incarnation.

Our individual matrix is the underlying structure that holds the holographic projection of our Lightbody. When we work with the Lightbody, we are also working with the multidimensional interactions of the individual and the Grand Matrix.

The Incarnation Grid

We work with a grid or field we have labeled the Incarnation Grid. Our sense is that this layer contains organizing instructions and expressions that help us to maintain our earthly activities in alignment with the objectives and goals for this incarnation. Numerous clairvoyants and psychics have detailed accounts of a pre-birth planning process that we all participate in. We enter this incarnation with an agenda or outline of the people we will meet and the lessons we want to learn. It is not tightly scripted and leaves room for free will and experimentation. This outline for the incarnation is somehow energetically coded into this grid structure. We do not think of working in this layer of information as working in the

Akashic Records, although there is possibly some overlap. At this point we have not been guided to use that terminology and have not specifically worked with the Akashic Records.

This grid communicates with our Core Essence, universal energy fields, and group consciousness to bring information and occurrences into our life that are in resonance with the grid's frequencies. Synchronistic meetings, sudden insights, and other supposedly "random" events can get organized through communication with this grid. Life events and thought expressions appear to create clutter or distortions in this grid structure. Sometimes completion of major goals or spiritual openings can create possibilities of new goals or realignment of the grid structure.

When we work with the Incarnation Grid structure, it is always with the help of our guides. The guides provide filters or cleaning hoops that we use to "comb" through the grid. Sometimes it feels as if it is just being cleaned up. Other times it feels that a new structure is being added. Greater clarity of this grid allows greater access for us to align with our life's purpose.

The Soul Field

Another field we have labeled and work with is the Soul Field. We have sensed that this field or grid is an organizing structure that mediates the interconnection of body and soul. Our sense is that there is a quantum-level communication connection to the High Heart Portal. We work with this field in the same manner that we work with the Incarnation Grid. Using filters provided by the guides, we gently pull them through this field. Here, changes to the field are generally more subtle, but noticeable shifts in the field and connections can be perceived.

Within the Soul Field, we may unconsciously hold soul fragments of another person, or others may have left aspects of themselves with us. These fragments generally do not serve our highest good. So as the guide brings the filter in, we can invite all the fragments we are holding to be released and returned to their sacred home. Additionally, we may have left aspects of ourselves elsewhere or have given them to another to hold. When the guides bring in the filters, we can invite all aspects of ourselves to return to us that are for our highest good.

Additional Fields and Grids

Most discussions of our HEF tend to focus on fields and grids that appear to be beyond the five senses, primarily because they are external to or outside the physical limits of our bodies. We also believe there are organizing energetic structures within the body. The generally accepted scientific theories place responsibility for operating the physical structure with our DNA. DNA holds the instruction set for making all the cellular and molecular components we need to maintain life. However, those theories omit the role of consciousness in the regulation of life.

Fascial Grid

One internal grid structure we work with is the Fascial Grid. Fascial tissue forms uninterrupted cellular sheets from head to toe. It weaves through and envelops every cell, organ, and body structure. The fascial tissue binds together structures, creates compartments to hold and transport fluids, and maintains our physical shape. It plays a role in almost every aspect of bodily function. Furthermore, fascial tissue is electrically conductive and may be the "internet" of the body.

We think that the true nature and importance of fascial tissue—and the Fascial Grid—is only now beginning to be understood by the scientific community. Recent years have provided a plethora of new discoveries related to fascial tissue.

We believe that the fascial system is an internal grid structure that is part of the electromagnetic HEF. Fascia may be the primary interface between the multidimensional aspects of consciousness and physical manifestation in this earthly plane. Our sense is that the Fascial Grid is communicating with the multidimensional HEF on a quantum level. There seems to be a strong quantum connection between the Fascial Grid and the Tan Tien aspect of the Hara.

Tim shares an account of one of his first experiences in sensing a distinct Fascial Grid.

This experience came shortly after my mother died while I was present in the room. My mother's Spirit/Soul had stayed around the room outside her body for a little over an hour after her breathing and heart had stopped. With a small ritual, she moved on, as most Souls do. It was after she left the room that my father asked me what I was sensing. So I walked over to my mother's body to sense and describe for him what I perceived.

I sensed a distinct energetic field around the body that felt more physical than spiritual; it clearly was not the spiritual portion of her. I was curious, as I had never separated this field out from the rest of the HEF in an animated body. A sister that was present also confirmed this energetically.

Then, a few hours after death, as family members were still in the room visiting, my sister noticed an energetic "pop." I checked, and the field had disappeared. Whatever was holding that field within the body had suddenly released.

Other Organizing Grids or Fields

Our sense is there are many other fields or grids that comprise our energetic structure. As we evolve and ascend, we will probably gain greater awareness of the existence and importance of additional aspects of our energetic structure.

The Primary Cell

To best convey the idea of the Primary Cell, we draw on the concept from the works of Grant McFetridge and Cyndi Dale. The simple version of the concept is that at conception, our everyday sense of self is formed. All of that awareness is consolidated and encoded in the Primary Cell. Just after conception, the fertile egg that becomes us starts to divide. After the fourth cell division (16 cells), the Primary Cell forms. This cell stays somewhere in the body all our lives.

The Primary Cell resonates with the vibrations of the universal matrix to keep us in sync with our birth intentions. However, this cell would also obviously be encoded with the genetic makeup from our ancestors. Trauma in this life or our ancestors' lineage can cause epigenetic disruption to the cell. This trauma (past lives, ancestral, and present) disrupts the ability to fully resonate with our Divine plan. These disruptions create epigenetic shifts and can cloud the cell's communication ability and therefore our capacity to fully achieve our potential. Healing of the Primary Cell reactivates its ability to communicate and our ability to achieve our full potential.

When working with the Primary Cell, we find that it can be anywhere in the body, although it is often in the upper body near the heart. Prior to working with the Primary Cell, we take care to elevate our frequency and come from a grounded and loving presence. The process we have used involves holding our cupped hands above the heart area and inviting the Primary Cell to energetically come into our outstretched hands. Rarely is there any resistance from the client's Primary Cell. It usually jumps right into the palm of our hands, ready to accept the healing work. In the rare times it is reluctant, patience usually pays off as it comes to realize the safe, loving presence being offered.

We often will sense that the Primary Cell is obstructed by some sort of binding, trauma, or neglect. We have gotten images such as an old sea chest, wrapped in chains and barnacles. Or a cell wrapped in webbing. There are a variety of ways the cell presents, and occasionally, it is radiant. Usually, however, some level of cleaning and releasing is needed to support the Primary Cell to come into full radiance.

We ask that all binding and obstructions melt away. Once the cell becomes free and clear, we set the intent to gently move and activate the core DNA of the Primary Cell. Depending on the type of healing protocol being used, we fill it with light and let the specific intentions and frequencies of that protocol do the work. Our intentions are always for the client's highest good so that the Primary Cell is able to reach its full potential.

Chapter Five

Working with Personal Energetic Boundaries

Being aware of our own energy is of key importance to stay in a centered relationship with self and to be in a healthy relationship with others. The first step is self-awareness, as every reaction is about us and not about the other person. If you get bothered by another person, it is always an invitation to look within and explore what your energetic habits might be. When we can bring that awareness not only into the mind, but into the body and then the energy system, we can recognize more of our "wholeness." This heightened awareness allows us to release old energetic expressions and adopt new ones.

We each have an individuated energy field. This energy field protects us from the world and yet allows us to relate to the world and beyond (multidimensionally). As stated previously, we know that the energy field is an unseen aspect of who we are. This aspect regulates the inflow and outflow of energy that supplies the impetus to be fully manifest in physical form. We are energy, and we are physical bodies.

When you can notice how far extended or how close your energy field is in relation to your physical body, this supports a deeper understanding of how you interact with others and how you are feeling inside. Many times, you may pick up on another person's "stuff" if you are extended too far energetically. On the other hand, if you "run your field" too tightly or close to your body, you may tend to have less contact with the world around you.

Depending on their environment, sea anemones may become large when feeling safe, just as when in danger or feeling threatened, they may "shrink" or pull in their body. It is instinctive for them.

We, too, have instinctual and unconscious "motives" or awareness-es that regulate our energy system. We can support how we are in the world and what we choose to create by bringing our awareness to the conscious level of understanding.

Furthermore, our energy system can be regulated to support us more deeply. You can create less drama and trauma in your body and life as you bring your awareness to the conscious level. Your energy body can serve you just as your physical body can. Developing the skills to enhance and strengthen your energetic being can make life smoother and more joyful.

One of the tools we use in bringing awareness to assessing our own energy field is by placing a small hula hoop on the floor. Step into the hoop and consciously bring your field to the size of the hoop. Begin to notice what you are feeling. Some questions you can answer:

- When you stepped in, did you step to the front or the back of the circle? (Don't move, just notice.)
- Are you feeling safe in a circle this size?
- Is your energy filling the hoop in all directions? If not, where is it different?
- Are you comfortable in it? Is it familiar to you or foreign?
- What are the physical sensations you are having? Do you want to run away or sit down, or are you indifferent to it?

Stay in the hoop for 3–4 minutes. Write down what you noticed. Now try with a larger hoop and expand your field to the size of the larger hoop (you can also use a string for this exercise by making a circle with it). Revisit the questions above—what are you noticing? Stay in the circle for 3–4 minutes and write down all that you noticed. All of this information can support you in understanding how comfortable you are and what size energy field feels secure for you.

Awareness is key in learning how to regulate your own energy body.

We often continue explorations using the hoops. Experimenting with interactions between people using different size hoops or overlapping hoops can provide additional insights into how you manage your field.

As we work with an awareness of a more expanded energy system or HEF, including all the grids and fields and multidimensional aspects of ourselves, creating healthy energetic boundaries becomes even more important. As we work with raising our frequency, broadening our view of connecting at higher levels with our Core Essence, and transmuting trauma within the physical body, we tend to get triggered less and less by others "invading our space."

Chapter Six

Sacred Geometry and Color Elements

Sacred Geometry is an ancient concept that describes the unifying and organizing principles of geometric and mathematical expressions in our world. The energy of creation arranges and organizes itself in specific, repeating expressions. Consciousness or Divine principles create the underlying sacred geometric expressions of life. Each specific geometric expression has its vibrational resonance or frequency. The frequency of specific expressions can be used in the practice of healing arts. The frequencies of a geometric shape can aid in the shifting, moving, and focusing of energy, helping accomplish the healing goals of bringing harmony and balance to the human energy system.

This section discusses some of the geometric expressions we use in our healing work. This book is not meant to be a treatise on sacred geometry. For more in-depth details, we suggest finding other sources.

Triads

The number three is associated with the trinity and completion. Three is often associated with wisdom and harmony. Biblically, and still in modern use, we often repeat phrases three times. We believe that there is power in the number three and find our work as a triad is much more powerful and fruitful than working in pairs or singularly.

Merkaba

The Merkaba is considered by many sources to be a Lightbody vehicle used to connect with and reach higher frequencies. It is also known to be multidimensional, allowing access to other planes of existence. It is

used as a tool by Archangel Metatron. A
Merkaba is based on a series of triangles.
Think of it as two entwined tetrahedrons,
one pointed up, the other down. Each tetra-
hedron is a pyramid with a triangular base.

We use the Merkaba in many ways. When
working with the earth and land, we visualize one or more large Merkaba bringing
in healing energy to shift local frequency.
We also use the imagery in the body when working with the Chakras
and other healing uses. Additionally, we often visualize ourselves
within a Merkaba while meditating.

When we work together, we see ourselves as part of a bigger Merkaba.
Our triad becomes connecting lines, forming the base triangle and
connecting with Christ Consciousness to form the upper pyramid.
Our angelic guides connect and join with Gaia to form the lower
pyramid, completing our Merkaba. The Merkaba is a powerful sacred
geometric expression that can be used in many ways.

Metatron's Cube

Metatron's cube is a sacred geometry symbol that has many meanings. The name is
somewhat misleading in that it is not really
a cube, per se, but a geometric pattern that
holds all underlying platonic solids. These
shapes combine to create all geometric
patterns of the universe.

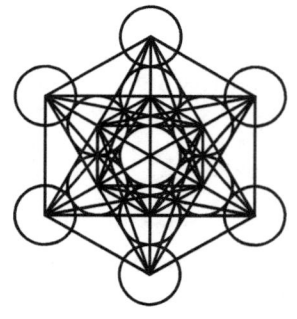

The shape of Metatron's cube begins with
the geometry of the flower of life. To draw
the cube in 2D, take the inner 13 circles of
a flower of life pattern and connect the centers of all the circles with
straight lines. Those lines create the outline that we think of as the
symbol of Metatron's cube. In 3D, the cube becomes more complex
and contains within it all other platonic solid 3D shapes.

This symbol has long been a sacred symbol in Judaic and then
Christian artwork.

There are many interpretations of the symbology of this shape, which is said to embody the flow and balance of energy throughout the universe. It is used to represent the archangels, alchemy, magic, balance of masculine/feminine, and much more. We encourage curious learners to explore the meanings and complexites of this sacred geometry by looking to other sources. There has been much written about this shape by authors more steeped in sacred gecmetry knowledge.

When we draw upon this symbol in our work, we visualize it as a 3D shape, usually spinning. We use the flower of life pattern as a protective shield, and we perceive the "cube" to be a tool wielded by Metatron to clear and heal our energetic systems. We specifically call upon Metatron to use this tool to repair and transmute flaws in our Hara. We visualize this spinning "cube" as a glowing and flashing geometric shape that slowly moves through our Hara, healing as it goes.

Möbius Strip

A möbius strip is a continuous one-sided surface. A simple way to understand this shape is to take a piece of ribbon, twist it a half rotation, then loop it back to itself and tape it back together. If you were to imagine an insect crawling along the surface it could continue to travel along the ribbon without ever finding the end. Möbius strips are typically made with a single twist, however, they can also be made  with multiple twists. Möbius strips are not typically found in nature but are commonly used in industrial or mechanical machinery.

In our work, we energetically connect Chakras or other parts of our energetic anatomy using möbius strips. This serves to balance, connect, and harmonize those energies and potentially boost the combined energy of the connected parts. We think that a möbius strip can function in multiple dimensions. We often visualize these möbius strips in figure eight shapes, although they don't need to be in that shape to be effective.

Möbius Coil

A möbius coil consists of multiple möbius strips. In the physical world there are numerous examples of people building möbius coils made of wire, which is achieved by continuously looping wire and twisting each loop as a möbius strip. These copper möbius coils will generate scalar waves.

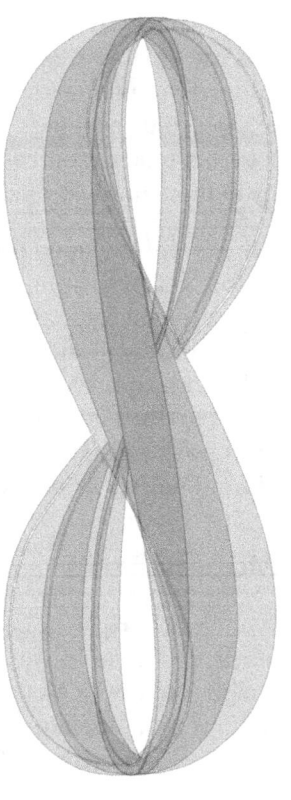

In our work, we create energetic möbius coils by visualizing a series of möbius strips linked together to make a structure, often surrounding a person or a portion of their body. Möbius coils serve to amplify the energy, provide protective coating, and are pathways to accessing quantum fields.

Labyrinth

Labyrinths come in many sizes and designs. Labyrinths have been found in numerous unrelated cultures dating to antiquity. The exact uses and spiritual meanings of the ancient examples are subject to much interpretation. Unlike a maze, the labyrinth has a single narrow path from opening to center, following a circuitous route to the middle. Many current uses of labyrinths are as an art form or an instrument for meditation and contemplation.

The energy concentration in a labyrinth depends very much on the intentionality of its design and construction, the frequency of use, and the mental state of the individual when walking it. Much like a church building resonates with the collective devotion of the faithful, a labyrinth holds the frequency of its walkers. We have found labyrinths to be useful tools to focus and quiet the mind in preparation

for spiritual guidance. The slow, meditative walk to the center prepares oneself for an inner journey. Once in the center, we are prepared to open to guidance and communion with the spirit word.

Some of our best inspirations and information have come from sessions in a labyrinth. Franny built a labyrinth on her Colorado property. Many of our early inspirations came in the space of that labyrinth. When creating any labyrinth, careful intentions in building, continued purity of thought, and sacred reverence creates an energetic form that allows that level of spiritual access.

Working with Color Frequencies

Color is vibration. In the color spectrum of the rainbow from red to violet, red vibrates at a more dense/lower frequency, whereas violet vibrates at a less dense/higher frequency, and the other colors range in between.

Each Chakra has a color associated with it that, in turn, holds that frequency. We can support our energy system by noticing which Chakra may be compromised and bring in that corresponding color frequency to strengthen a particular area.

In 2018, our guidance asked us to begin to work with a higher frequency of colors for the Chakras. As we listened, we began to experience the upgraded frequency of iridescence fusing with the Chakra colors. Red became iridescent red; orange, iridescent orange; and so on with all the colors. This shifted the frequency to allow for more expansiveness to the energy system.

One of the teaching tools is to experience and play with colors. Starting with your Root Chakra, bring red color into your hands and your whole being. Hold this color frequency for a minute or more, sensing and experiencing the color. Then add iridescence and notice any changes. Try one by one with each of your Chakras with the appropriate color.

Rays or Ray of Light

"Ray of Light" is a title given to a specific or focused aspect of the consciousness of our Creator. The consciousness of the Creator pervades the entire universe. The various Rays of Light are different frequencies of the same one light: the energy of pure, Divine love that subtly guides and informs our reality.

In our usage, light is information. Each Ray is already part of our Soul, waiting to emerge. The Rays of Light are a form of teaching this information—they are a discipline or study of Divine light. Each Ray has an associated luminary or master. We can ask for the guidance of those masters and luminaries to assist in our work and our personal growth. One only needs to ask for their assistance, and they are ready and willing to help.

Crystal Grids

Crystal grids are an arrangement of crystal stones aligned in sacred geometric shapes or other alignments that serve to amplify the intentions for healing or manifestation. There are potentially an infinite number of possible grid arrangements. We do not consider ourselves the experts in this arena, as there are many other resources available to help deepen the knowledge for those interested. Our discussion here serves to describe how we have used crystal grids to support our work and in our client practices.

We seem drawn to the frequency of various stones and have plenty of rocks around the house. We find certain crystals or combinations of them to be beneficial for certain clients or situations. We rely on our guidance when deciding to include crystal grids in our workshops and retreats. Some workshops have included grids as part of the protocols, whereas other workshops have limited the use to experiential activities.

Often the crystal grids will be built with a center crystal and an array of supporting stones arranged in a pattern around the center. The center stone serves to both anchor and amplify the frequency of the intent. The surrounding crystals communicate with the center crystal and augment or amplify the center frequency. All crystals should be in alignment and supportive of the frequencies and intention of the work.

In previous workshops, we used crystal grids as an evening group experiential. This group activity allowed unstructured "play" time to allow participants to experiment and sense the energetic interactions with the crystals and grids. Through play, they were able to sense how the crystals shifted energy patterns in different arrangements. The groups were able to follow the wisdom of the stones in deciding arrangements. If attention is given to the crystals, they will show you how to arrange themselves.

Chapter Seven

Working With
Spiritual Guides

Our experience of the natural world is similar to some of the ideas expressed in the theory of evolutionary cosmology. That school of thought believes that the entire universe is constantly in a state of evolution, rather than purely in mechanical motion dictated by the laws of physics, and that creative evolution co-exists within the laws of physics yet is guided by layers of consciousness.

Everything exists in nested morphic units, similar to a fractal. Whether it is particles, atoms, molecules, cells, tissues, organisms, societies, planets, solar systems, galaxies, or universes, at every level, things all exist as both a whole and a part of some larger structure or organization. Even respected physicists such as Rupert Sheldrake are finally starting to theorize that perhaps there is guiding intelligence at every level.[2]

Our cosmology follows this train of thought. We believe that there are intelligent forces that guide all aspects of our creation. Those guiding forces, like all matter, are part of expanding hierarchies of organization, intelligence, and consciousness. All those levels of intelligence can be both the guide and the guided.

So, too, with us. As co-creators in our world, our spirits are quite powerful, yet we can access far more power if we tap into the vast array of guides at every level of creation. There are legions of angels, guides, and beings throughout the galaxy and universe. We are at once both a part of and the whole of this entire universe. Our

2 Sheldrake, Rupert. (2009). *Morphic Resonance: The Nature of Formative Causation*. Park Street Press.

evolution as humanity on this planet is deeply intertwined with the evolution of the entire universe. As such, much of the rest of the universe is rallying behind our growth and evolution. As we move forward, so does all of creation. For this reason, we have many helpers at all levels of the galaxy and beyond who are eager to aid if we would just ask.

The following section details some of the many guides that we are aware of who aid in this work. It cannot possibly be anywhere near complete as we are probably only aware of a small fraction of the many levels of guiding intelligences. As our awareness continues to expand, we keep getting pleasant surprises as more benevolent beings are revealed to us.

We want to add a note of caution here. There are many beings and forms of consciousness in the universe. We think of categorizing them in three different segments. Some are benevolent and eager to help humanity. Those in this group recognize the concept that we are all simultaneously separate yet a part of the whole. With that recognition, they know our advancement is also theirs, and they willingly support this common path forward.

Another segment is in a sense neutral, operating on their own agenda, unaware of our common oneness. Sometimes they are useful when our agendas agree. At other times they seem to be in our way, but they are just operating on an agenda that, at the moment, conflicts with our agendas. Perhaps one could think of them as competing for the same energetic resource, which they assume to be limited. One needs to be careful with this group as they could help today and hurt tomorrow.

The third segment (we think a small percent) are actively involved in working against humanity. This is as true in the human community as it is in other forms of consciousness. In the human world, we would not willingly share our credit cards with just anyone, only those we have determined will keep our best interests in mind. Much the same as working with humans, one needs to practice discernment when working with these beings.

We have found that the best way to practice discernment is to *only* work with those beings that you have discerned and/or identified are working for your highest good and that of all humanity. This is done by coming into one's heart space, being grounded into the Pure Timeless Earth, and connecting directly to Source. Then you ask that the information presented—or the beings that are bringing the information forward—is of the highest frequency of Divine light. Holding oneself in a high frequency state of being supports getting an accurate answer.

We would like to make note here that *all* the benevolent beings that are helping with our work are of the Source/Creator. It is always our intent to bring forth the Creator's highest frequency of love— the Christ Consciousness light—in this and all dimensions.

Angelic Realms

This book is not meant to be a treatise on the many realms of angels. There are many other resources available to the inquiring reader that define the specific roles each of those groups of angels assumed to aid as messengers of the Divine and helpers in this world. Similarly, there are many resources that give expanded details about any particular angelic entity. Note that we do not believe that angels have a gender. They may appear as male or female, and though we often use a gender-based pronoun based on the common presentation, they are gender neutral.

We are only given a small glimpse of these guides and how they appear as they offer us assistance. They often show up or appear how we want to see them or in a costume that makes us feel safe. It is our belief and experience that the angelic kingdom is at our service if we would only ask for help. All sincere and altruistic requests for help will be met with an instantaneous response. They seem quite happy to be of service and are honored that we ask for their help. They are bound by this request; however, they must operate within the limits of their rules of engagement and laws of the universe. Angelic and Etheric Beings are not limited by space or time and have the ability to be in multiple places or dimensions simultaneously. Additionally, they always respect the free will of humans to make good or questionable choices.

Specific Guides and Helpers

Christ Consciousness is the awareness of the presence of God/ Creator/Divine at the heart of everything in creation—every atom, being, plant, rock, animal, sun, moon, and all matter and consciousness. We hold to the value and heart-centered knowing that the Christ Consciousness is the purest presence of Divine love, gratitude, and compassion.

Janet Mentgen was the founder of Healing Touch and created a way to bring hands-on healing work to the earth in a more mainstream fashion. Her goal was to have healing hands in every home, school, and hospital. Her strong curricular program created the template of a five-level foundational energy medicine program for the world. She passed away in 2005 and continues her work from the other side. Janet has supported the Awakening Healing Axis collective by being a guiding light from the etheric realms.

Archangel Michael is mentioned in both Old and New Testament books as well as the Quran and seems to be well known to people we have met in the "eastern" world. He is portrayed as both healer and protector. He is often shown with a sword and in cobalt blue colors. We invoke his protection and oversight of our work. He frequently appears in his warrior form, standing guard in healing sessions or when dealing with difficult energies. His softer healing aspect is calming as he infuses that cobalt blue frequency through our nervous system. We see him as a constant companion in this work.

Archangel Metatron appears in Hebrew and Kabbalistic texts as one of the highest of the angels. He had a human incarnation as Enoch before ascending into an elevated status in the angelic kingdom. He is usually depicted with his sacred geometric form of the Metatron cube, which contains all the platonic solids, symbolizing the building blocks of life. He supports our work in a variety of ways, raising our frequency. We specifically call on him to support the transmuting and maintenance of our Hara.

Archangel Uriel is considered one of the major angels in religious texts. Uriel is the leader of the Seraphim and helps with healing resentments and forgiveness. Uriel shows up in both gender forms and in red and golden colors. Uriel will step in when called and often appears waiting to be invited for those situations where that frequency can best transmute the stuck energies.

Archangel Raphael is known throughout most Abrahamic religions as the angel of healing. He is one of the archangels always invoked in this healing work. We see him associated with an iridescent emerald green color that can be used to open, transmute, and heal. We often invoke and incorporate the healing frequencies of Raphael's presence into the healing sequences.

Archangel Gabriel has a number of biblical appearances as the messenger of God and protector of truth and righteousness. We experience Gabriel as a strong protective force and brings a very soothing energy. Gabriel shows in both gender forms, with an iridescent golden yellow light that wraps us in warmth, love, and peace. Gabriel heals with a frequency of light, releasing, relaxing, and calming, and is also very useful in calming the nervous system and releasing traumas.

Archangel Raziel shows up in Hebrew texts as the keeper of the secrets and mystery. He is often depicted holding a sacred geometric form. We find him to be quite playful and joyful, bringing in an iridescent frequency of rainbow colors. He often operates as a cosmic level alchemist, transmuting any barriers in multiple dimensions. When we opened to his support, this work shifted into a higher frequency, opening new doors. We often ask him to bring in the iridescent rainbow frequencies to clear and transmute.

Archangel Jophiel is considered the angel of beauty and wisdom. When working with us, she presents as an iridescent fuchsia frequency. She supports our work in holding a Divine remembering of the beauty and light that we each are directly from Source. Many times, she will appear with her fuchsia mist to surround and bring protection and stillness.

Archangel Zadkiel is considered the angel of mercy and leader of the dominions. He can be invoked as a healer for trauma and mental challenges. Zadkiel brings in the frequency of a deep, iridescent indigo blue. He serves with Michael as a leader in battle and captains the angelic Knights Paladin for protection and healing.

Knights Paladin is a powerful group of angels. They appear as male warrior knights. Some of us hear the sounds of their armor as they arrive. Usually 12 of them appear with Zadkiel when invoked, but at times there are more of them. They are a powerful protective force that can be called upon. They are also powerful healers able to transmute in multiple dimensions. Their healing work often involves the use of sound or toning to transmute and balance.

Divine Wisdom we refer to as a leader, and the embodiment of the Divine Wisdom energy. She appears as a feminine warrior, holding the feminine aspect of the Christ Consciousness. The Divine Wisdom frequency is an iridescent magenta. She holds a powerful ability to support and command the Magenta Warriors in protection and healing.

Magenta Warriors are a feminine counterpart to the Knights Paladin. They are powerful as a protective force and also marvelous healers. They resonate with the frequencies of Divine Wisdom energy and are amplified with the use of shungite crystals. They also utilize toning in concert with the Knights Paladin for healing.

Rahanni are a high frequency angelic and celestial group bringing in the iridescent pink frequency. They are a commanding presence when they arrive. They are great protectors as well as healers. When they are invoked, we often sense them come in suddenly as a powerful column of pink light. When protection is desired, they form a perimeter around the area needing protection. When in-voked for healing and transmutation of energy, they are softer, yet powerfully transmute energies and provide sustaining force to enable the healing to hold.

Ascended and Illuminated Masters support the work and the common ascension of humanity and the planet. The Ascended Masters are a collection of guides that have all completed their incarnated work on the planet. They continue to learn and grow as they support us all in positions of the spiritual hierarchy. They all have specific areas of responsibility and work with certain frequencies. They will appear as needed and respond when invoked.

Another group that aids the work is referred to by us as the **Iridescent Masters**. This group of high frequency beings supports the iridescent frequencies and helps to maintain high frequency in our personal transformations and healing work.

Many Beings at All Scales help this work. From the atomic level to the galactic level, there are benevolent intelligences that are helping our common ascension. At the smallest scale we have been introduced to a group we affectionately label the Comet Beings. These beings zip around at the atomic and molecular level, looking like little comets. They seem to come and go as they traverse the multidimensional landscape of the micro-level world. They are willingly invoked to assist in transmuting energy throughout the physical body.

At the earth level, the cetaceans that roam the oceans are advanced intelligences that support the ascension of the planet and all her inhabitants. They can be invoked to participate in healing work and often transmute energy using sound vibration or toning.

The elemental kingdom of nature spirits is also a resource for healing. They can access many different healing frequencies. As in all things, discernment is especially important with this group as their trust in humans is not uniformly high. They have their own agenda and may not always be in alignment with ours.

There are beings and intelligences available at the planetary and solar level that can be called upon when needed. These groups are especially useful when working with large scale energy disturbances related to space and time.

We have also been working with a group we term the Star Beings. They do not self-identify as originating in any particular star system. Their work has been related to bringing in a certain frequency of energy that we sense as a yellow-orange metallic color and high frequency. This frequency is particularly useful in working with the Lightbody and Matrix level healings.

There are many other galactic-level intelligences that come to our aid to create the highest frequencies sustainable in the healing work.

Guides and Crystals can work together to enhance the frequency. We have found a number of crystals to be useful for anchoring in and amplifying the frequencies of the guides. Shungite in particular seems to have opened a gateway into higher frequencies and associated helpers. Our sense is that shungite has been made popular in recent years as part of a grand guided plan to distribute it around the world, enabling a realignment of the planetary grid. The unique crystalline structure of shungite serves well to amplify the frequencies that are being brought in through this work.

When setting a crystal grid, we often start with shungite in the middle and then choose support crystals. Sometimes color is important in the supporting crystal; however, the basic defining quality is frequency. We have used a number of different supporting crystals. Black tourmaline is a favorite, along with quartz, varieties of amethyst, more shungite, and several others. The guides asked for several different stones such as anyolite, rhyolite, and dragon stone to support the "dragon" energy frequencies. The yellow amethyst (citrine) supports the "Star Being" frequency. Calcite has also been supportive for the higher frequencies and shifts in planetary alignment. Use your intuition to choose the crystals to support your individual needs in each moment. Experiment with different grids and configurations that resonate with the most supportive frequencies for you.

Chapter Eight

Role of the Heart in Healing

The heart is the doorway to the love we are all being asked to remember—that we are the gateway to Divine remembering and connection with the Christ Consciousness. In all of our work, we focus on the power of the heart! The toroidal field that emanates from each person's heart expands and fortifies with greater force to strengthen us as humans living within a physical body.

The heart is the bridge between the physical and spiritual realms, inviting us to *be* the love of the Divine here in physical manifestation. It is through embracing the love of the Universe that we may be a clear vessel of light for ourselves, one another, and truly all of humanity.

All high frequency healing is done from a pure heart and Divine connection, allowing us to become conduits for love to flow through and with us as we work with the highest frequencies of guidance and support.

> *"The heart communicates to the brain and body through hormones. In 1983, the heart was reclassified as part of our hormonal system. One of the hormones, atrial peptide, helps to reduce the release of the stress hormone cortisol. As such, we have a chemical communication going on between heart and body all of the time. However, this is where things get really interesting. The heart is an electrical organ producing by far the largest amount of electrical energy in our bodies—40 to 60 times as much power as the second strongest organ, the brain. This heart energy permeates every single cell in our bodies. The signal is so strong that it creates an electromagnetic field (toroidal) that surrounds the body in*

360 degrees and can actually be measured up to three to four feet outside the body."[3]

When we increase coherence, stress levels go down, brain function improves, and we have the ability to feel positive emotions that regenerate us. This all leads to more awareness, intuitive discernment, and the ability to live a more heart-centered life.

Focusing the breath within the body, connecting to our heart, mind, Source above, and the heart of the earth allows us to be present and *be* that conduit for the Christ Consciousness. We strive to hold the template for each person and each participant of our workshops to fully remember that they are here to support themselves and the collective of humanity to bring about the great change we all have the power to contribute to.

3 McCraty, Rollin. (2015). *Science of the Heart, Volume 2: Exploring the Role of the Heart in Human Performance.* HeartMath.

Chapter Nine

The Making of a Workshop

All our workshops follow a similar template. We believe it is important to ground our work in scientific principles and earthly knowledge, and to acknowledge the limits of this understanding. We then present our understanding, which usually goes well beyond the bounds of currently accepted scientific thinking. This is important as energetic work can only be partially explained by current scientific models, though science validates the work more than most people realize. Additionally, there are especially useful real-world analogs to energetic practices. Visualization is an important aspect of high frequency work, so it is important that we provide some platform of visualization to more gracefully allow the practitioner to make the leap into the multidimensional space of the high frequency work.

Workshop Preparations

Anyone who has put on a workshop knows there is a lot of logistical work and planning that goes into creating a successful event. This work requires the same attention to detail that any workshop would require. In addition to the usual, we think it is important to take the time to energetically prepare on multiple levels prior to the workshop. We meet a few days prior to our workshop to make sure we have all the materials and presentations ready for the event. We also work to prepare the workshop space and the participants. Well in advance in the planning, we "visit" the retreat center grounds in our meditations and together during our phone conversations, preparing the land and working with the energies of the space to clear the area for our work. In the few days before the retreat, we again do guided work to open and clear the land. During our preparations, we have been visited by Native American Guides and others that come to help us honor the land.

We also believe it is important to energetically connect and attune with each of the participants prior to the workshops. To aid this process, we ask each participant to send us a picture and write a page or so of background in response to some questions posed about the workshop. We take the time for our triad to sit with each participant's paper and attune with them. In that process, we get insights into the needs of the various participants, noting that perhaps some subtle energetic shifts will be needed. Most importantly, we are each more aware of what each person needs and how to be attentive to their energy and interactions during the workshop. We believe that the moment someone commits to a workshop, they energetically link up into the group and start preparing at a higher level of consciousness.

An excellent example was reported to Tim after a one-day workshop. A participant who had never met Tim said that shortly after she signed up, Tim began appearing to her in her dreams. Over several of her dreams, she was given all the information she would receive in the workshop, although she did not realize that was happening. The day of the workshop, she was in amazement as everything we taught was just as she recalled from her dreams. This level of connection and aware- ness may not be the norm, but we think that it is happening on a subtle level for everyone. We are always connected far beyond our normal level of thinking and understanding.

Labyrinth Ceremonies

We feel that it is important to start and end each workshop with a ceremonial ritual. The labyrinth seems the perfect vessel for that ritual. We always need to work with the local conditions and physical limitations of each labyrinth. Additionally, some places do not have a labyrinth. In those cases, we adapt the ceremony while retaining as much of the energetic characteristics as possible. Unique but similar ceremonies precede each workshop. The opening ritual has more than meets the eye and is designed to catapult the participants into the extradimensional space of the workshop.

As each participant steps into the labyrinth, they step onto the Merkaba symbol and repeat a phrase that opens an energetic door, shifting their energy system to be more receptive to the higher frequency teachings. Of course, each individual shifts in a way that mirrors their personal readiness and openness. Some who are fully ready are catapulted into extradimensional space; others shift more slightly. As they walk into the labyrinth, the group recites a mantra. Each workshop uses a mantra designed for the energies of that time. Many guides, representatives of the Native American elder's council, and elementals grace our presence and welcome us into the space.

We have a similar "bookend" ceremony to complete the workshop physically and energetically in the labyrinth. The closing ceremony is designed like the opening. Rather than opening to new concepts, the closing ceremony affirms and anchors the teaching. The participants all recite a mantra similar to the opening, although it is worded to be a fulfillment and embodiment of the ideas expressed. As they leave the labyrinth, they step on the Merkaba symbol and step out of the energetic envelope that helped them for the duration of the workshop. The closing ceremonies are always filled with spiritual helpers, guides, and elementals honoring the light and awakening of all participants.

Sometimes participants are surprised to see how grateful and thankful the guides are. The guides are always eager to be of assistance but are seldom asked to serve in this manner.

Workshop Experientials

The following two exercises are included in the workshops to allow the participants to experience the power and frequency of forms that would otherwise be merely intellectual constructs. Most of us need to experientially sense something before we can understand it. We have found that this is especially true for energetic sensations that are beyond the normal five senses.

The Merkaba is a sacred geometry pattern, yet many people have no experience with that pattern. The torus is a common energetic phenomenon that is part of the human energy system, yet most are unaware of it. These exercises help to make the patterns more tangible and to anchor an understanding of these energetic concepts.

Merkaba Exercises

As noted in the previous chapters, we consider the Merkaba to be an important sacred geometry element in this work. The Merkaba is much more than a geometric symbol—it is a powerful energetic gateway to accessing and using the higher frequencies available to us. Energy frequencies need to be experienced for us to remember and reproduce them. It is quite helpful to have an intellectual understanding, but it is only through the experiential that we gain the knowing that we seek.

The following describes the exercises we use to allow participants to begin to experience and integrate the power and energy of the Merkaba. Ideally this exercise is done in groups of seven. It can also be done in a group of four, although it is less effective. Facilitators not only direct the activity but involve themselves in creating the space, directing and amplifying the flow of energy for maximum benefit. The design of this activity allows everyone to experience the interior energy of the Merkaba as well as be part of creating the energy lines and flow of energy within the Merkaba.

Note: It is important to be aware that occasionally there are participants that find the energy too intense or have difficulty with balance while in the center. Using a chair in the center would be slightly safer; however, it puts the center person at a lower elevation than the rest of the group. We have had only a few such instances in the many experiences with this exercise. In one instance, a person with inner ear balance issues could not tolerate the position in the center of the Merkaba and needed to stop. Another incident occurred where the person in the center dropped to the floor, unhurt, as they were caught by the group. In that particular case, it was actually healing. The energy was so intense that a non-beneficial energy that had been residing in them exited, causing them to momentarily lose balance.

The setup for this exercise is to create groups of seven. Ask one of the group volunteers to start in the middle position. The other six people arrange in a circle around them. The next step is to get every other person to hold hands together, creating sets of triangles. Getting people situated correctly for this part can be a little confusing. (See following diagram.) It works best if one person from each group of three is appointed as group captain to help direct the spin direction of the subgroup.

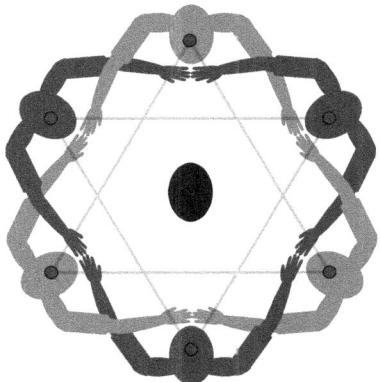

All of the spinning and energetic movement is created on the level of intent. The groups are not actually moving during the exercise. One triangle (group of three) is asked to visualize connecting their triangle of energy with Christ Consciousness above. This creates an upward facing pyramid, which they will spin clockwise. The second triangle visualizes connecting below to the Divine Essence of Gaia. This creates the second downward facing pyramid, which this group of three will spin counterclockwise (as viewed from above). Once everyone understands their role and energetic assignment, the group is directed to focus their attention on the creation of the Merkaba and spin in the appropriate direction.

The intentionality creates the energetic form of the spinning Merkaba with high frequency spiritual support. The person standing in the middle of the spinning Merkaba experiences the full energetic power of this dynamic sacred geometry. It is an excellent way to feel that frequency with the full body and get a glimpse into the power and potential. We use Christ Consciousness and the Divine Essence of Gaia as the two spiritual ends of the pyramids. Other guides or angels could be used as well. If the exercise is done as a group of four, then three spiritual helpers will be needed to complete the circle of six and create the Merkaba.

Allow the groups to experience the frequency and energy of the Merkaba spinning for 1–2 minutes. Then the group is directed to slow the spin and stop. Switch out the person in the middle. When the switch happens, be mindful of the group captain role, making sure each subgroup knows who the captain is. We find it best to switch direction of the spin. The triad that was spinning clockwise shifts to counterclockwise and vice versa for the other triad. This gives everybody a chance to experience all roles and minimizes dizziness.

Repeat the Merkaba spinning experience for another 1–2 minutes. Continue the process until all seven participants have been in the middle position.

Follow up with sharing of the experience. Everyone will have a unique experience. It is fascinating to hear the different awareness of the energy and the range of experiences that are articulated. This experience creates a building block to energetically understand an element of the frequency shift process.

Torus Experience

We have used variations of our torus experiential as the last workshop exercise prior to completion. Having discussed the torus conceptually during the workshop, most participants have an intellectual idea of the torus as a fundamental shape of Chakras and energy bodies. As with most energetic concepts, true understanding is accomplished when we can grasp it both intellectually and feel it with our sensory facilities. This exercise creates a large energy torus with the group, which enables most participants to sense and understand the power and flow of energy within the torus.

Creation of the torus is quite simple. The group is divided in half. One half is directed to create a circle, holding hands together. This group will be spaced close to each other. The other group is directed to make a second ring, surrounding the first group. The second group spaces at arm's length apart. This arrangement now makes two concentric circles. Each group is then directed to create a flow of energy in their circle. The inner circle flows energy clockwise (as viewed from above), while the outer circle flows energy counterclockwise. This creates a large energy torus that is usually felt by even the least sensitive member of the group. The feeling is quite powerful.

The experience can be repeated by reversing the direction of flow and noting the difference. The inner and outer groups can also switch places and experience the torus from another perspective.

Chapter Ten

High Frequency Shift

If you have read our previous work, pay extra attention to this chapter and the small but important changes to the High Frequency Shift (HFS). As we acclimate our systems to increasing energy flows, the guides continue to make adjustments, allowing ever greater connections to high frequency energy. We consider all of these techniques to be a work in progress, making frequent tweaks and adjustments.

Previous work referred to the Advanced High Frequency Shift (AHFS) as a higher frequency version of the Basic High Frequency Shift (BHFS). We are now moving beyond the BHFS, so we are dropping the reference to "Advanced," only having one version, which will be called the High Frequency Shift (HFS). In our workshops we tend to add the upgrades to the HFS. When we do, we go over the changes step-by-step to entrain that upgraded energy into the participants' energy bodies.

We believe the HFS is one of the important keys to accessing the highest frequencies now available on the planet. There are a lot of small steps to the process, and it may seem complicated at first. Listening to the guided versions of the HFS on our web-based Learning Center is a good way to get used to it without getting bogged down in remembering the steps. With practice, it becomes second nature and can be done quickly. When proficient, one can sequence through the steps in just a few moments. When we voice-guide meditations, we typically take several minutes. When learning, going through it slowly allows one to fully experience and integrate the depth of energetic shifts at each step of the process. One may also realize that the more they practice, the deeper they go.

The biggest change we've made to the HFS is our connection to the planet. Previously we used the concept of the "new earth" or transmuted earth to connect with. This allowed us to connect to the evolving or ascending version of our planet. There are many groups of people on the planet working on ascension. Most are doing good work, but in different ways and often with different messaging. When tuning in to this variety of work, it seemed like an orchestra out of tune. Not all are at the same frequency, so the "new earth" felt discordant.

We were guided to the concept of the "Pure Timeless Earth Template." This concept is the potential pure earth that resonates out of the pure Divine Matrix. Once we started connecting into the Pure Timeless Earth, the energies became purer and more elevated. We also found that some high frequency people who had difficulties connecting to the planet did better. These advanced souls could not connect into our distorted earth but could connect into the Pure Timeless Template of Earth. This has important implications when working with the flood of enlightened souls that are now incarnating. The Vivaxis connection is also shifted when the Pure Timeless Earth is substituted for the current earth connection.

Invocation/Intention

The first step is to invoke our spiritual guides. Include your personal guides as well as the angelic helpers. We invite in different spiritual helpers depending on the type of work we are doing. We almost always invoke archangels Michael, Gabriel, Raphael, Uriel, Metatron, and Raziel. In addition to these six, many others will be situationally called upon. We particularly also invite in the Christ Consciousness frequency/energy for Divine support. It is also important to set the intentionality of the work you are doing, whether you are doing a healing session or just your daily energy hygiene.

The first level of intent we always set is that all will be to the highest good at this time. This overarching intent is important, and it also inherently acknowledges that our conscious minds cannot begin to comprehend what that possibly means. Our limited understanding of "highest good" needs to be put aside to allow for the unfolding of a much grander plan. We may also have some secondary intentions for our session, such as healing emotional or physical pain.

Protection

The protection step focuses on creating sacred space within and around us for our work. The first step is to envision yourself connected to the Divine Source. How we do that can be very individual as we all have different notions of what Divine Source means. This needs to be your personal connection to "God," the universe, or some higher power. One simple way to visualize that is having a power cord connecting us to the Divine. Just plug in that cord!

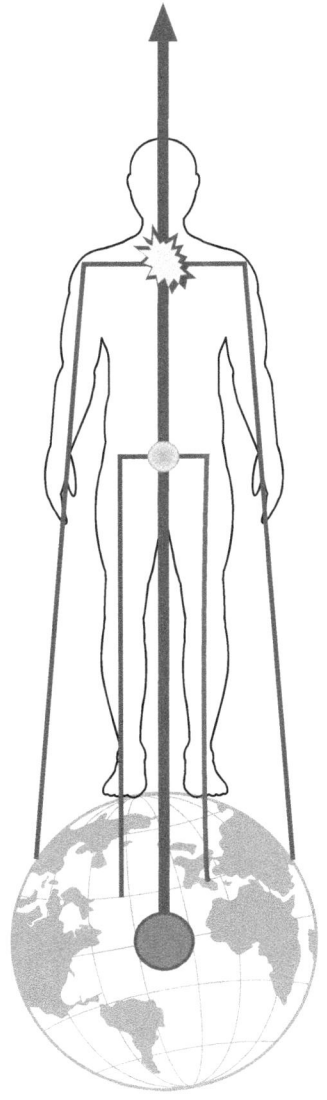

Once connected to Source, we visualize a coating of pure white light that flows over and surrounds us, covering like paint. If working with a client, cover them with the same protective layers as well. Follow the white layer with a coating of iridescent rainbow colors. Cover that layer with a coating of gold glitter, sparkling all over you. We then bring in an element of sacred geometry. Visualize yourself being surrounded by a protective bubble. The bubble has the geometry of the flower of life and shimmers with iridescent rainbow colors. We hold this protection in place as we work with the energy system of ourselves and our clients.

Hara Attunement and Anchoring

Attuning, anchoring, or setting the Hara activates that vertical line of energy that exists in the dimension of intentionality and focuses our connection to earth and purpose in life. We begin by tuning into the zero point of the Pure Timeless Earth. We are connecting to the Divine template of a pure potential that may be in the emerging future. This version of the planet has the highest frequencies possible to align with our evolving human consciousness and our energetic ascension. It is also important that your Core Crystal connecting deep within the earth is upgraded and polished, allowing the crystal to resonate with and hold higher frequencies.

We begin by putting our awareness at our Tan Tien in the lower abdomen. From the Tan Tien, visualize a line of energy connecting down to the very center, zero point of our planet. Anchor that line of energy from the Tan Tien to your upgraded Core Crystal. Consciously connect and merge your Core Crystal into the crystalline matrix of the Pure Timeless Earth. Visualize your Core Crystal aligning with the grid structure of this pure earth, becoming one with the earth. Allow the frequency of Divine earth energy to flow up your connection, filling your Tan Tien.

Bring your attention to the Soul Seat, located just above the Heart Chakra, and draw that Pure Timeless Earth energy into your Soul Seat. Next, focus on a point above your head, allowing the Pure Timeless Earth energy to flow straight up through the top of your head and connect to your point on the Divine matrix, and the energy of the Universal Source. Pause a moment to sense the connection to Divine energy below and above. Visualize a column of light running vertically through you.

Optionally, you may focus on expanding and strengthening the Hara connection. Expand by connecting the energy from the Tan Tien out to your hips, then down your legs, connecting deep into the earth. Sense your Hara column of light growing as wide as your hips. Next, focus on the Soul Seat, sending the Hara energy out to your shoulder joints and down your arms, connecting deep into the earth. Pause to sense the feeling of a stronger, wider Hara. You are now connected by five lines woven into the earth's grid lines and matrix, deeply anchored to the core of the earth and to the universe above.

Vivaxis Transmuting/Healing

Bring your attention to Vivaxis. Think of a hose-like connection from your left foot off to a place in the earth somewhere near where you were born. Imagine a small sphere of light in the earth where it anchors. Connect the matrix of the sphere into the matrix of the Pure Timeless Earth. Sense the quality of that connection and the flow of

energy. Ask your guides to transmute
anything that distorts or blocks the flow
of energy in your Vivaxis. Imagine it
filled with swirling, iridescent colors of
the rainbow or the colors that allow it to
flow most freely. When that connection
feels clear and flowing, visualize those
colors flowing up your leg, dispersing
into a vapor as they rise up your thigh.

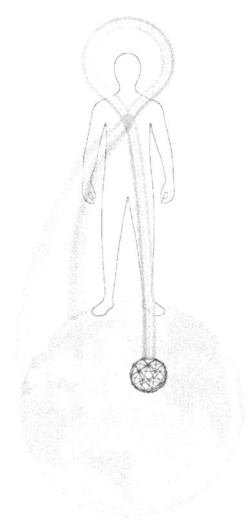

Allow that flow of colors to swirl up
across the left hip, through the torso on
the front side, crossing the heart and up
toward your right shoulder. The colors
swirl around your head then down the
back side, again crossing the heart and
exiting through the entire right side of
your body, connecting back to the earth. This process may be slower
the first few times you do it. With regular practice, you will find your
Vivaxis is normally pretty clear, and it goes quickly.

When the energy flows more aligned, you may sense an interaction
between your Vivaxis and your 10th Chakra. The 10th Chakra contains
information about your connection to the planet. As your Vivaxis
expands with the gridlines and matrices of the Pure Timeless Earth
allow a resonance with your 10th Chakra. Release anything in the 10th
that does not serve your highest good at this time.

Hara Transmuting/Repair

We believe that Hara repair is best done by our angelic guides, and
Metatron is our "go-to" guide for this exercise. Metatron uses the tool
of his sacred geometric shape, Metatron's cube, to recondition our
Hara from the inside out. For this step, ask for Metatron's help.

Metatron uses a double cube. A larger version of the cube will
descend through the inside of the Hara, rotating as it goes. A
smaller version of the cube is connected to the larger cube. As the
large cube rotates inside the Hara, the smaller cube rotates as it
transverses the outer wall of the Hara. This combination of cubes

repairs, renews, and transmutes the inner and outer wall of the Hara as well as all internal structures.

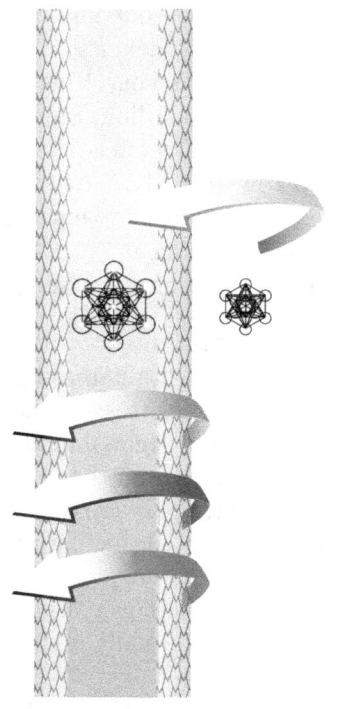

We ask that Metatron transmute and repair the Hara to the best condition possible today. As he does the Hara work, you may experience different sensations as your energy shifts. Sometimes it seems that his cubes stay in one place for a long time. This is usually in areas where the energy is not flowing well, and much repair work is needed.

Envision Metatron inserting his spinning cubes into your Hara above the head, with the cubes spinning clockwise. As the cubes slowly descend, you may sense that they move faster or slower depending on the amount of repair work needed. The double cube slowly works down the Hara column, out below the feet, and down to the core of the earth to the crystal where you anchor. There it reverses direction, spinning counterclockwise and moving up the Hara until it passes above your head. The cubes then reverse direction again and make a second pass, slowly descending, spinning clockwise, then back up again counterclockwise. The second pass is usually a little quicker as most of the work is done on the first pass. Occasionally, a third pass will be needed.

After Metatron has completed the work, invite Archangel Raziel to fill your Hara with a tapestry of golden and iridescent rainbow light, infusing your Hara with the highest frequencies you can hold. Next, we ask that the Quantum Hara Points be re-ignited and woven together with a double figure eight möbius. (The Quantum Hara Points are detailed in Chapter 15)

Now that the inner work is complete with the Hara, the Magenta Warriors come in at the base of the Hara. Swirling clockwise with an iridescent magenta energy, they spiral up the outside walls of the Hara, polishing and cleaning. When they reach the top of the Hara, a Divine anointing oil flows down, coating the outer walls of the Hara, which creates protection and sealing of the outer structure.

Pause and sense your renewed and brilliant Hara.

Chakra Fusion, Expansion, and Unification with Hara

The Chakra fusion, expansion, and unification step focuses our attention on each of our in-body Chakras sequentially 1st–7th. This focus expands and clears the Chakra, raising its frequency as it expands. As the Chakra expands, it flows into the Hara, unifying, fusing, and blending colors into the structure of the Hara. When all seven in-body Chakras are unified and fused, we move to our highest frequency Chakra at the 12th and make our way to the lowest frequency out-of-body Chakra at the 8th. With this approach, we are following the same path your soul takes as it steps from the heavens and into the earthly plane. By moving closer and closer to our physical form through these out-of-body Chakras, we are experiencing how to bring our spiritual expression into unity with our physical self by drawing more and more of our soul light into our bodies.

Starting at the Root Chakra, imagine a ball of iridescent red light flowing into and filling the torus of the Chakra, expanding, and flowing faster. Allow it to fill and energize the Chakra, flowing faster as it spreads and clears, fusing into the Hara structure. Allow time to deeply sense the Chakra expand and unify as the vivid red becomes one with your Hara. Set the intent that it will stay flowing at that higher frequency, unified with the Hara.

Bring your attention to the Sacral Chakra as you visualize an iridescent orange ball of light filling the torus of the Chakra, expanding, and flowing faster. Allow the orange light to expand and fuse the Sacral Chakra into your Hara. When the Sacral Chakra feels fully expanded and unified, keep it flowing and bring your attention to your Solar Plexus Chakra.

See an iridescent yellow ball of light enveloping your Solar Plexus Chakra, filling the torus of the Chakra, expanding, and flowing faster. Allow the yellow light to expand and fuse the Solar Plexus

Chakra into your Hara. When the Solar Plexus Chakra feels fully expanded and unified, keep it flowing and bring your attention to your Heart Chakra.

Imagine an iridescent green ball of light enveloping your Heart Chakra, filling the torus of the Chakra, expanding, and flowing faster. Allow the emerald green light to expand and fuse the Heart Chakra into your Hara. When the Heart Chakra feels fully expanded and unified, keep it flowing and bring your attention to your Throat Chakra.

Visualize an iridescent sky blue ball of light enveloping your Throat Chakra, filling the torus of the Chakra, expanding, and flowing faster. Allow the blue light to expand and fuse the Throat Chakra into your Hara. When your Throat Chakra feels fully expanded and unified, keep it flowing and bring your attention to the Brow Chakra.

See an iridescent indigo ball of light enveloping your Brow Chakra, filling the torus of the Chakra, expanding, and flowing faster. Allow the indigo light to expand and fuse the Brow Chakra into your Hara. When your Brow Chakra feels fully expanded and unified, keep it spinning and bring your attention to the Crown Chakra.

Imagine an iridescent violet light enveloping your Crown Chakra, filling the torus of the Chakra, expanding, and flowing faster. Allow the violet light to expand and fuse the Crown Chakra into your Hara. When your Crown Chakra feels fully expanded and unified, keep it flowing and notice how all seven Chakras are flowing—with their brilliant iridescent colors filling the Hara—and your energy frequency feels elevated.

Once the in-body Chakras are fully flowing and unified, visualize them fusing with each other and creating an aligned column of pulsing power.

Now bring your attention out to your 12th Chakra, the Golden Matrix. Visualize iridescent golden colors swirling into the outer edges of your energy body, activating and raising your frequency. Notice the flowing and expansion of the 12th Chakra as it weaves the energetic shell to unify the Hara with all the Chakra colors and energies.

Shift your attention to the 11th/Connective Chakra as you visualize iridescent, metallic blue colors flowing into your hands, feet, fascia and through the energy fields. Feel the frequency of the 11th Chakra flowing and fusing with the Hara.

Move your attention about 18 inches below your feet to your 10th/ Earth Star Chakra. Imagine an iridescent earth tone ball of energy flowing into and filling the torus of this Chakra, expanding, and flowing faster. It expands and unifies with your Hara, spreading the iridescent earth tones through the Hara.

Bring your attention to the 9th/Soul Star Chakra about 18 inches above your head. Visualize iridescent copper colors swirling and filling the torus of your 9th Chakra, sensing as it spreads and flows faster. As it flows, it expands and unifies with your Hara, spreading the copper colors through the Hara.

Continue the Chakra expansion as you turn your attention to unification with the 8th/Gateway Chakra. Visualize iridescent silver light flowing into your 8th Chakra a few inches above your head. Sense the filling of the torus of the Chakra, expanding and flowing faster. Invite the fusing into your Hara.

Sense how all 12 Chakras are unified and stacked along the central channel of the Hara. Vibrant, fused, flowing, and expanded at a high frequency.

Core Essence and Hara Expansion

The following description is a slower and deeper version of Core Essence expansion. We recommend that you periodically use this slow version as it allows for deeper clearing and heightened sensitivity to the amount of "stuff" we carry in our energy field. We do not need to carry that unnecessary baggage, and we can learn to travel lighter through our daily lives. With repetition and practice, you can move through the expansion in a few breaths.

Bring your hands over your heart space. Sense deep within the core of your being, connecting with your Core Essence. Imagine your Core Essence as a brilliant blue-white star deep in your body. Acknowledge that Divine spark that is your true self. As you focus on your Core Essence, visualize your star getting brighter and expanding into every cell of your physical body. Feel it light up your entire being.

Using your breath, as you exhale, continue to slowly expand your Core Essence beyond the boundary of your skin, out into the 1st layer of your energetic body. Core Essence lights up and clears your etheric body layer. Expand your Hara so it, too, fills the space of the etheric body.

As you inhale, imagine your Core Essence drawing back to a point of light deep within. On your next exhalation, slowly expand your Core Essence out into the 2nd layer, your emotional energetic body. Sense it light up and clear your emotional body. Let Core Essence dissolve all the emotional energy that you are holding in this 2nd layer. Pause here for a breath or two, if needed, to fully clear this layer. Be aware of the calmness that comes. Then expand your Hara so that it now extends out to the edge of your emotional body.

Again, as you breathe in, imagine your Core Essence drawing back to a point of light deep within. Exhale and slowly expand your Core Essence out into the 3rd layer, your mental energetic body. Sense it light up and clear your mental body. Let Core Essence dissipate all the thought forms and mental energy that you are holding in this 3rd layer. Pause here for a breath to fully clear this layer and sense the clarity of a revitalized mental body. Then expand your Hara so that it now extends out to the edge of the mental body.

Breathe in and draw Core Essence back to a point of light deep within. Exhale and slowly expand your Core Essence out into the 4th layer, your astral energetic body. Sense it light up, clear, and vitalize your astral body. Pause here for a breath, if needed, to fully clear and sense this 4th layer. Then expand your Hara so that it extends out to the edge of your astral body.

Inhale and draw Core Essence back to a point of light. Then, exhale and slowly expand Core Essence out into your 5th layer, the etheric template energetic body. This is the blueprint of your physical body. Let Core Essence light up and flow through all the lines and grids of this layer, clearing and vitalizing your etheric template. Pause here for a breath to sense the difference in this 5th layer. Next, expand your Hara so that it extends out to the edge of the etheric template layer.

Breathe in, drawing Core Essence back to that point of light deep within. Breathe out slowly, expanding your Core Essence out into the

6th layer, your celestial energetic body. Sense how iridescent colors flood and expand your celestial body. Pause here for a breath to experience your brilliance. Expand your Hara so that it fills to the edge of the celestial body.

Again, as you breathe in, Core Essence draws back to a point of light. Next, exhale slowly to expand your Core Essence out, fully extending and vitalizing your 7th layer, the ketheric energetic body. Pause here for a breath to sense the difference in this 7th layer. Expand your Hara to the edge of the ketheric body.

Breathe in, drawing Core Essence back to a point of light. Exhaling slowly, expand your Core Essence into the field associated with the 8th Chakra. Sense how the 8th layer becomes more vibrant. Now, expand your Hara to the 8th field.

Breathe in once more, and Core Essence draws back to a point of light. On your next exhalation, slowly expand your Core Essence out, filling the field of the 9th Chakra, vitalizing that layer. Expand your Hara with Core Essence to the 9th field.

Breathe in, drawing Core Essence back to a point of light. As you exhale, slowly expand your Core Essence into the field associated with the 10th Chakra, vitalizing this layer. Now expand your Hara to the 10th field.

Again, as you breathe in, Core Essence draws back to a point of light. Next, exhale slowly and expand your Core Essence out, filling the field of your 11th Chakra. Expand your Hara with Core Essence to the 11th and Fascial Grids.

Finally, breathe in and draw Core Essence back to a point of light. As you exhale, expand your Core Essence out, filling the outer layers of your energy body and 12th Chakra. Expand your Hara with Core Essence to the outer extent of your energy bubble.

Core Essence lights up the golden bubble of energy that surrounds you. Hara fills and expands into your entire energetic being. Feel the pure, full expansion and remember this feeling so you can come here often. Hold Core Essence in this expanded state.

Bring Hara back to a size that feels comfortable to you. This may change over time, and it may be situational. Most people find that a

Hara expansion of three to four feet feels right. When going out in public places, most people are better served by having a more compact energy body. Only if you have practiced good, clear boundaries should you have a large, expanded field in public places.

Core Essence Elevation

Elevation of our Core Essence is a key part of accessing the higher frequencies now available. This description is for a slower version, which is essential when first learning and wise to use occasionally if you are able to put this into practice. It has been our experience that once Core Essence is elevated, it is like unlocking access to the frequencies. Core Essence will tend to stay elevated if practiced regularly. If not lovingly cared for, it will drift back to our old, lower frequency.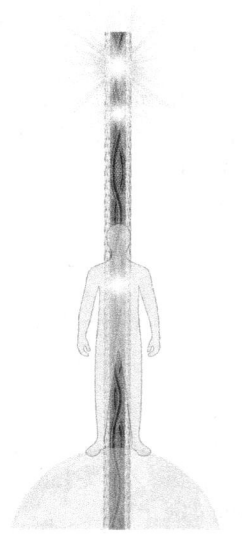

Following the expansion of Core Essence, bring your hands to your chest, holding them over your heart space. Connect into that spark of Core Essence. Simultaneously connect into your Oversoul, which resonates with the highest frequency of your soul in this plane. Visualize the connection between Core Essence and Oversoul. Let your Core Essence rise to the highest level it can reach.

Take notice of the elevated frequency and give your Core Essence permission to reside in this new home space.

High Frequency Shift: Client

The High Frequency Shift (HFS) for the client is very close to the previous versions described in our other books, with a few additions included. The first is to include clearing of the client's Vivaxis, which was not part of the earlier description.

When working with the client's Vivaxis, hold one hand on the bottom of their left foot and the other palm facing out below their foot. Focus on the sphere where the Vivaxis is connected to the earth. Ask the guides to help. Ask that the sphere connection be shifted to connect with the Pure Timeless Earth, which will give it a higher frequency connection. Visualize it connecting to the earth grids and crystal matrix of the planet.

Next, focus on the connection between the sphere and the left foot of the client. Work with the guides to clear any blockages or distortions. They may use any range of colors or elements to clear the flow. When good flow is established, check to see that it flows through the body optimally. Again, use the guides to assist as needed.

When flow feels strong, moving to the head of the treatment table (seated is easier), place both hands on the client's Crown Chakra. Focus on your own Core Essence, maintaining frequency as high as possible. Invite Metatron to come through you, spinning a double cube and entering into the client's Crown Chakra, spinning clockwise, and descending down the Hara. Ask Metatron to transmute and repair the Hara as much as possible at this moment. You might sense that his cubes stay in one place for a long time. This is usually in areas where the energy is not flowing well and much repair work is needed.

The double cube slowly works down the Hara column, out below the feet, and down to the core of the earth to the crystal where the client anchors. There it reverses direction, spinning counterclockwise and clearing up the Hara until it passes above their head. The cubes then reverse direction again and make a second pass, slowly descending, spinning clockwise, then back up again counterclockwise. The second pass is usually a little quicker as most of the work is done on the first pass. Occasionally, a third pass will be needed.

After Metatron has completed the work, invite Archangel Raziel to fill the client's Hara with a tapestry of golden and iridescent rainbow light, infusing the Hara with the highest frequencies they can hold.

Now that the inner work is complete with the Hara, the Magenta Warriors come in at the base of the Hara. Swirling clockwise with an iridescent magenta energy, they spiral up the outside walls of the

Hara, polishing and cleaning. When they reach the top of the Hara, a Divine anointing oil flows down, coating the outer walls of the Hara, which creates protection and sealing of the outer structure.

Next, move along the client's body, near their Throat Chakra. Bringing your awareness to the client, visualize or sense where the client's Core Essence vibration rests. Most people have the Core Essence between heart and throat. If they have done this work before or have a strong spiritual practice, it may be higher. Gently invite the client's Core Essence to rise in frequency. Using your hands, encourage their Core Essence to move toward the Throat Chakra as the frequency shifts up. Partial movement is okay if it is slow to respond.

Holding your hands above their Throat Chakra, visualize a Merkaba forming above the throat in your cupped hands. Invite the client's Core Essence to rise up into the Merkaba. Visualize Core Essence as encapsulated in the Merkaba.

Slowly move your hands and the Merkaba up over the client's face until it rests above the Brow Chakra. Pause at that position to allow time for Core Essence to come to equilibrium at the brow. Many people sense a restructuring or rewiring that happens as the Brow Chakra adapts to the higher frequency of Core Essence. When it has stabilized, slowly move your hands to the top of the head above the Crown Chakra. Hold that position for a while to allow time for the crown to integrate and stabilize. You or the client may again sense rewiring or energetic shifts as Core Essence adapts to this new location. Set the intent that Core Essence can now reside above the crown at this higher frequency.

Part 2

Spring 2023 Workshop, St. Johns, FL

Divine Delight:
Exploring and Embodying Your Soul

Chapter Eleven

Creation of the Spring 2023 Workshop

Following our normal patterns, we told our guides not to download information for future workshops and retreats until we wrapped up the retreat in front of us. Translating the information we get into teachable segments that we can present in this linear world always takes more time than we wish. Although always intrigued by new information, we try to keep our team organized and focused on the task ahead of us.

As soon as we wrapped up the previous (Spring 2022) retreat, we started the listening process to figure out what was coming next. Sometimes it all comes rushing in at once; sometimes it comes in dribbles. This time we were told that the guides were purposely holding some information from Franny and Tim so that others on the team would be pushed to listen and gain confidence in their participation. We included a team training workshop after the 2022 retreat for mentoring those who stepped up to help build AHA and support moving this work into the future. During this time, we allowed space for some of the new material to come through.

As we worked together at the AHA team retreat and preparation workshop, new frequencies appeared in the form of guided meditations and energy work for us all to partake in. Specifically, the color frequencies of chartreuse and opalescence were experienced. Some shifts within the team's energy structures appeared as the new frequencies came through. Layers of Hara that had been hidden from our awareness were revealed. This set in motion months of experiments and meditation by the team as these new revelations worked their way into the fabric of the next workshop.

Embodiment of our Divine origins was one of the key concepts that needed to come through. It seemed that all participants desired to know their life purpose or path. Deeper embodiment offered a path to that understanding. Through guided group brainstorming, we added ideas and topics to be included in the planning. We felt that self-love so significantly influences all the concepts we cover that it would need to be a recurring element of all workshops going forward. It was also noted that "self-love" seems to be overused and well worn, so new words and ways to express that concept needed to be woven into the work. The information we were getting showed us that we needed to provide a deeper level of experience so those participating in our workshops could become more self-aware of their Chakras and energy bodies.

We were also gathering that we would need to revisit and work deeper in the fascia systems. Some new thoughts about working extradimensionally with fascia had come through the previous autumn and were slowly percolating in our awareness and practices. "Dancing with the fireflies" came in as one of the themes for the workshop. This metaphor would pop up in numerous ways during the planning process as we were nudged to notice aspects of this in books and information we were exposed to.

We worked as a larger team to focus the ideas and weave them into a coherent curriculum for the five days of workshop time. We met periodically as a team and separately in triads as the ideas wove themselves together into the unified fabric of the workshop.

Mirrors

The idea of seeing the outside world as merely a reflection of our inner state is based on the notion that how we perceive the world is heavily influenced by our beliefs and emotions. We retained some of the mirror concepts used in the previous workshop but primarily used the mirrors as a tool to look deeper into ourselves. We suggest you use a mirror to practice some of these exercises at home.

We recognize that it may be difficult for some people to look at one-self in the mirror. If that is the case for you, go softly with yourself and try to look at the inner beauty instead of the outside reflection. As you gain a deeper appreciation for your true inner self, you may find more acceptance of the outer self and allow the years of false programming to slowly slip away.

Journaling

We provided journals for each of the participants and encouraged them to journal throughout the workshop. We normally do this for our workshops; however, during this particular workshop, we allowed more time for journaling as the topics invoked deeper personal exploration and pondering.

We suggest that you may also wish to journal or take notes as you read along, as we encourage you to undertake the same process of self-exploration. After each of the new sections or experiential exercises, take the time to make notes on your thoughts and reflections. This may allow you to dive deeper into your process of self-revelation.

Chapter Twelve

Opening Invocation: April 2023

We began the workshop in ceremony, using the following invocation to set the frequency and intent for the following days. The ceremony included a ritual to join as a group and move into multidimensional awareness. We typically use a labyrinth in the opening ceremony. This time there was not a suitable labyrinth available, so we found a spot in a grove of trees for the simple ceremony. Participants and presenters all stepped onto a symbol of a Merkaba as they entered the opening circle. They were guided to recite the phrase: "I step into this time and space, opening my awareness to all possibilities." As they recited the phrase there was an energetic interaction to shift them into an elevated energetic frequency. Once all had entered the opening circle, the invocation was spoken slowly as a group two times through, allowing time to process it and integrate the statements of the invocation in between statements.

Divine Delight: Embodying Your Soul

I step into the template of the Pure Timeless Earth, fusing my awareness with the crystalline matrix of our planet.

I inhale deeply and draw its powerful energy into and through me, activating my entire being.

I honor the ancestors, elementals, and benevolent beings embodying and protecting this and all sacred land and water. I am at ease in the safety they offer.

I welcome new shifts in my inner awareness, inviting deeper remembrance and presence in my being of the pure love that is my sacred self.

I open my arms and embrace the Divine light of Source,
inviting my luminescence to ignite, letting it fill me as
Source radiates from me.

I breathe in, opening and inviting new Divine frequencies
of pure love to flood through me as I embody all aspects of
my sacred self.

I release all limited ideas of self and reality. I am open to
embracing all quantum shifts within my being as my soul
invites embodiment on this lifetime's journey.

I embrace new potential for awareness of personal boundaries
and compassionate energetic interactions with others.

I surrender to serve the Divine plan, embracing the highest
possible frequencies and dimensions flowing through me,
allowing these frequencies to purify and amplify all aspects
of my being, accelerating self- and planetary-ascension.

I fill myself with gratitude and awe, opening my soul to its
luminous place in the fabric of creation.

My heart expands as I connect with the Divine masculine
and feminine aspects of the Christ Consciousness and to
my Oversoul, as I awaken.

Workshop Experientials

The experiential portion of the workshop is where the amazing energy
of high frequency does its work. Through these experiences, the participants have the opportunity to both give and receive the work. All of the
following exercises are done as an energy healing trade. Participants
pair up. One assumes the role of the practitioner while the other takes
on the role of the client or recipient of the work. We refer to the person
receiving the work as a client. When on the table receiving the work,
powerful healing experiences can happen. Often, people have reported
profound, life-changing shifts. The practitioner may also have profound
experiences as a witness to the multidimensional healing energy flow.
After the session is complete and time is taken for discussion and reflection, the participants reverse roles so that both have an opportunity
to give and receive.

This exchange anchors in the frequencies and allows the participants to remember and reproduce the sessions after the workshop. Some participants have healing practices and will replicate the work with their clients, spreading the frequencies and healing. Others may be participating primarily for self-healing. Self-care versions of the experiences are provided for all participants, allowing them to continue their healing self-care at home.

Our intent is set for the recipient's highest good at this time in their life journey. This is guided work. We ask for the highest frequency level of guidance needed that will help the recipient today. These sequences have many steps, so it is best to have this printed material in front of you to help when first practicing until the practitioner can do it from memory.

Self-Love: Bringing Self-Acceptance Through All Levels of Your Being

Based on experiences in the last couple of workshops, we have come to appreciate the profound impact and deep need to work on the concept of self-love. We now feel that it is such a core element that it is important to start with self-love. Some feel that the idea is a bit overused. However, though the term is in common use, the understanding and practice is poorly integrated. We have added some extra words to help add meaning and hopefully more integration. The extra words include thoughts about generosity to self, grace and forgiveness to self, valuing self, and treating self fairly. These are all thoughts we consider when interacting with others. The goal is to get across the idea that we should treat ourselves as well or better than we treat others.

The deeper we have worked with self-love, the more clearly we realize that the scarcity of self-love affects our entire world view as a society. In this workshop, we again used the idea of mirrors, similar to the workshop detailed in our previous book. We weave experientials throughout this segment to slowly open the doors to deeper self-realization. Participants were encouraged to journal their thoughts and experiences throughout the workshop. We encourage you to journal as you read along, too. We followed this first session with a table-based healing experiential with a partner to anchor the self-love energetically deep into the body.

Mirror of the Golden Rule

Stated in many different ways, the golden rule appears in biblical, Confucian, Zoroastrian, and other more recent writings. The golden rule is basically, "you should love/treat others as you love/treat yourself." Sounds easy. However, in practice, we often treat others better than we treat ourselves. How many times have we diminished ourselves in ways we would never consider treating others, even people we don't care for? The reality is that love starts with us. If we never develop love and appreciation for self, we can never fully love others.

We start with suggested ways to treat others well. This list also gives us a start at using other words to ask about self-love. The words in italics are used to further the exploration of self-love.

- Treat others with courtesy and respect and *generosity.*
- Be more empathetic and try to understand others, allow them *grace.*
- Don't belittle others, allow for *forgiveness.*
- Do not look down on others.
- Treat everyone *fairly.*
- Acknowledge the *value* of every person.
- Do not manipulate or deceive anyone.
- Think before we speak.
- Do not judge or negatively comment on physical appearance.
- Always acknowledge everyone as a whole person.

We begin by exploring our sense of self using a handheld mirror. We suggest the mirror as a reflection of our self-intimacy ("into me I see"). We ask the participants to gaze into their mirror for at least a full minute, then journal what they saw, sensing and being present to what emotions they felt. We encourage you to put down the book at this time and do the same exercise.

We suggest a mirror of the golden rule. Instead of "love others as yourself," change it to "love yourself as others." The first question to ask while gazing into the mirror for a full minute is: ***Am I as fair and generous to myself as others?*** After gazing and pondering that question, journal about your physical, emotional, and mental reactions.

Again, pick up your mirror. The next question to ask yourself while gazing into the mirror for a full minute is: ***Do I forgive myself as I would forgive others?*** After gazing and pondering that question, journal about your physical, emotional, and mental reactions.

Pick up your mirror again. Ask this question of yourself while gazing into the mirror for a full minute: ***Do I value myself as much as I value others?*** After gazing and pondering that question, journal about your physical, emotional, and mental reactions.

Taking up your mirror to gaze. The next question to ask while gazing into the mirror for a full minute is: ***Do I give myself as much grace as I do for others?*** After gazing and pondering that question, journal about your physical, emotional, and mental reactions.

We followed the mirror exercise with a description of the step-down process of our incarnation. At our deepest levels of Core Essence, we are pure and vibrate with the many frequencies of love. As our Core Essence lowers frequency to become soul and ultimately our physical manifestation, there is some distortion to the pure love. Further distortions get introduced as we navigate the world and create our belief system and worldview. That distortion affects our self-love and self-concept. The greater the distortion, the more challenging it is for us to express our love.

Ultimately, all expressions of our love get filtered through the lens of our self-love. If our lens is cloudy, less love is able to be expressed. A cloudy lens (low self-love) impacts all our relationships. It hinders beneficial thought expressions such as acceptance, compassion, and harmony. The cloudy lens feeds the low frequency thought expressions such as anger, pride, and fear. When we are low on self-love, we continually search for love outside ourselves. This perpetuates the illusion that we are separated from love. It hides the knowledge that we are, at our core, made of love; it is our true identity.

Using the filter and lens analogy, we offer this explanation of how we form our reality and reinforce the distortions of our self-love. The cycle in the next figure works to build and reinforce the distortions. Our beliefs and energetic expressions shape how we give our attention to the world around us. In this example, if we believe we are not worthy, we will diminish ourselves and pay attention to making sure we (mostly unconsciously) present ourselves as "less." Since we are paying attention to being "less," we will perceive how others notice us and treat us as "less." Emotionally and mentally, we will register those reactions of others, and it becomes our experience. The experience of being treated as "less" leads to internalizing that sense of worthlessness. That feeling reinforces and cements the belief that we are indeed not worthy.

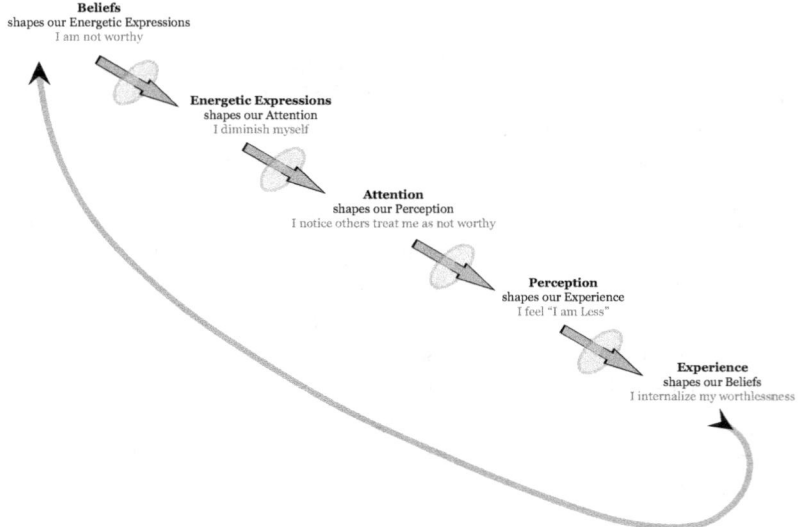

Beliefs
shapes our Energetic Expressions
I am not worthy

Energetic Expressions
shapes our Attention
I diminish myself

Attention
shapes our Perception
I notice others treat me as not worthy

Perception
shapes our Experience
I feel "I am Less"

Experience
shapes our Beliefs
I internalize my worthlessness

To compound the self-love problem, most of us spend our lives searching for love outside ourselves. Our perpetual search for love is based on the idea of separation. We search for the love that will make us whole, the love we missed in childhood, the love that seems just out of reach, our perfect companion. We look outside ourselves, but separation is an illusion. The love we seek is inside us. The separation we sense is the separation from self, from our identity, which is love.

All this begs the question: "How do we clear and purify the lens of self-love?" If only we can clear the lens of distortion, we can align ourselves with the pure love that is our Core Essence.

We suggest that clearing the lens in personal transformation is usually a gradual process. A clear lens comes from embracing and accepting all aspects of ourselves with awareness and self-love. Clearing the lens means letting go of the false narrative that we believe about our lack of love. Lens clearing is not easy, as it requires acceptance and forgiveness of self. Many of us seem to be at war with ourselves, but we don't need to fight ourselves about the parts we don't like. A clear lens brings greater joy, love, and compassion for self.

Affirmations are one of the tools that can be useful in clearing the lens. Affirmations are a tool to repeat and practice a statement until you can internalize and begin to believe it. Using the example in the previous figure as a guide to transformation, we can substitute the affirmation "I am Core Essence" for the belief "I am not worthy."

Energetically, that affirmation changes the energy we project, shifting our patterns and our attention. When we interact with others, they will notice that energetic shift and treat us differently and more respectfully. Our experience changes and our notion of reality improves. We begin to shift our belief system, which affects how we hold our energy, reinforcing the shifts in our reality. If we practice enough, we can master the thought and slowly clear the lens of distortions.

To begin this process of self-acceptance, we asked the participants to slowly go through this set of statements as a mantra:

- I am my Core Essence, in oneness with Divinity.
- I am in alignment with my Oversoul, supporting me to be love.
- I allow my Soul to shine through me and guide me as love.
- I know that my earthly appearance is an aspect of love.
- I compassionately accept my human limitations, knowing I am love.
- I fill myself with grace to act in love.
- I lower my walls of protection to accept love.
- I am love, and I am being love.

After this guided meditation experience, we ask participants to gaze at their mirrors again with awareness of their feelings and sensations. They were to ask themselves these questions:

- Can you see a glimpse of your Core Essence?
- Are you a brighter light?

After gazing, they were given a period of time to journal in their notebooks. We suggest you also take time to do the same.

Embodiment is another path to clearing the lens of distortion. Embodiment can be accelerated by:

- Inviting our Soul and highest aspects deeper into our being, opening space in our heart and High Heart.
- Acknowledging our connection to our Core Essence.
- Deeply desiring that our soul be embodied.
- Asking that we come home to who we really are.

We had the participants contemplate what embodiment means and take a few moments to journal those thoughts. We invite you to do the same.

Self-Love Healing Protocol (Experiential)

We followed the guided meditation with a break before explaining the experiential table work. The experiential is done working in pairs at a treatment table. One participant takes on the role of practitioner, the other the role of client or recipient of the work. After the session is complete and time is taken for discussion and reflection, the participants reverse roles so that both have an opportunity to give and receive. If possible, we suggest that you find a partner to practice this experiential.

Prior to working with the frequencies of this protocol, it is important to attune to the frequencies of gold that will be used in the purification process. We invite you to partake in this self-experiential, to attune yourself with the gold frequencies.

The first frequency used is white-gold. White-gold is the Divine masculine frequency of Source and Christ Consciousness. It holds the purity of the male aspect. To experience this frequency, take a moment to calm your system and center yourself. Hold your hands in front of your chest and visualize holding an orb in the palm of your hands. Invite in the swirling, Divine masculine frequencies of white-gold into the orb. Allow those frequencies to fill that orb, build, strengthen and pulsate. Bring that orb into your Heart Chakra and let the frequency of white-gold fill your heart. Notice the sensation and qualities of this frequency.

Next, we invite you to experience the frequency of rose-gold. Rose-gold is the Divine feminine frequency of Source and Christ Consciousness. It holds the purity of the female aspect of Divinity. Hold your hands in front of your chest again and visualize another orb in the palm of your hands. Invite the swirling, Divine feminine frequencies of rose-gold into the orb. Allow those frequencies to build and fill that orb. Bring that orb into your Heart Chakra and let the frequency fill your heart. Notice the sensation and qualities of this frequency.

Next, we invite you to experience the frequency of pure-gold. Pure-gold is the frequency of Source and Christ Consciousness. It holds the frequency of "The One." Hold your hands in front of your chest and visualize holding an orb in the palm of your hands. Bring in the swirling frequencies of Divine Source with pure-gold. Allow those frequencies to build and fill that orb. Bring that orb into your Heart Chakra and let the frequency of pure-gold fill your heart. Notice the sensation and qualities of this frequency.

Next, we want to experience the blending of these frequencies. Hold your hands in front of your chest again, visualizing an orb in the palm of your hands. Bring in each of the swirling frequencies of Divine Source with pure-gold, rose-gold, and white-gold. Allow all three frequencies to build and fill that orb, creating a triangle—the trinity. Notice the sensation and qualities of these frequencies. Bring that orb into your Heart Chakra. Allow the frequencies of white-gold, rose-gold, and pure-gold to blend and mingle, filling Heart Chakra and expanding into your High Heart Portal. Connect the Seat of your Soul with High Heart Portal. Ask your soul to come deeper into your body, ask your soul to allow you to know your true self, your Divine Essence, a projection of pure, unconditional love. For some people, the triangle of the trinity morphs into a Merkaba. Honor whatever sensations you experience.

The purpose of this technique is to:

- Clear and realign the mind, body, and spirit to support all aspects of one's Divinity to be an inner radiant Being of Light.
- Heal, strengthen, and integrate all physical, emotional, mental, and spiritual energy bodies.
- Facilitate restructuring and repatterning of self-love to create healthy cell regeneration.
- Release the charge of traumatic experiences that diminish our perception of self-worth.

- Sense and experience the power of higher frequency emotional memories.
- Enhance our ability to experience all forms of love as the distortion of self-love shifts.

Our goal is to reduce the distortions and align self-love with the pure love of our Core Essence. We will be using frequencies of gold, energetic releases, and affirmations to deepen the embodiment of our pure essence, which is LOVE.

The client will be lying face up on the treatment table for this protocol.

Step 1: High Frequency Shift—Self/Practitioner
The first step of the session is High Frequency Shift (HFS) for the practitioner. This is done while holding the feet of the client. The HFS brings the practitioner to the optimum elevated frequency to be the conduit for the client. It also serves to entrain the client in that elevated frequency, beginning the process of healing.

Step 2: High Frequency Shift—Client
The next step is to perform the client version of the HFS, ensuring the client is also at an elevated frequency.

Step 3: Distortions to Self-Love Memory Release
This technique serves to soften the energetic effects of memories that no longer serve us. It does not erase memory; instead, it releases the energetic binding of the memory, thus bringing more balance to regions of the brain affected by trauma. (Credit to Healing Crucible, LLC, originator of the technique.) We have included modifications to flow with the energetic frequencies of the entire protocol.

An important aspect to remember is that the energetic work is being done by the angelic guides. The practitioner is holding and being sacred space, helping create that opening for the work to unfold. When we do this, we often get imagery of angels flipping through a file cabinet of records, pausing now and then to clear a record. We also get little vignettes or images of past events. Clients at times may also get imagery as the past memories are processed. You may or may not get the visual imagery and may sense it differently. It is important, as the practitioner, to just hold space and do not get attracted to the images or story. The story is not important, the release of emotional energy is what is important.

Note: There are three separate hand positions to Step 3.

Visual Brain Access (1ˢᵗ Head Position)

Move to the head of the table. Position both of your hands under the client's head with your fingertips along the occipital ridge (the bottom of the skull bones). Your thumbs align on the back of head as close to the visual cortex as possible. The visual cortex is directly behind the eyes toward the back of the head.

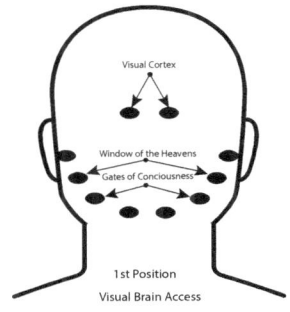

1st Position
Visual Brain Access

As we settle in that position, we invite the angelic guides to work. The guides will open access to the client's past experiences in this current lifetime as well as other timelines that serve this purpose. The guides will go through the memories to clear the emotional load of any memories that are no longer serving the client's highest good. The memories are not erased or altered, just the emotional load or trigger associated with the memory is released.

The practitioner will hold this position until the work feels complete. The process usually takes a few minutes. When complete, slide your hands out from under the head and move to the second position.

Connecting Frontal Lobes (2ⁿᵈ Head Position)

This hand position is done on the face. Place your thumbs on the frontal lobes, directly above the client's eyes. Your fingertips are placed along the bottom of the cheekbone. Your little fingers are placed next to their nose. The other fingers are spaced along the check bone with the index finger near the ear.

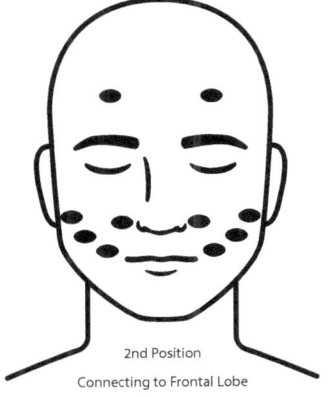

2nd Position
Connecting to Frontal Lobe

This position connects the energy into the frontal lobes, which are often shut down during traumatic events. We again invite the angelic guides to do the work as the practitioner holds sacred space. The practitioner and client may again get imagery as the guides do the work. This work feels different and usually a sense of calmness starts to come in. The practitioner will hold this position until the work feels complete. The process usually takes a few minutes. When complete, gently release and move to the third position.

Emotional Clearing (3rd Head Position)

This next position connects to the limbic and emotional centers of the brain. This helps clear the emotional link to the events. Your thumbs stay on the frontal lobes, as in the previous position. If you imagine a line that traces across the top of the client's head from ear to ear, that gives you the location where your fingers will be placed.

Begin with the little fingers just in front of the ear canal. As best as you can, place your remaining fingers spaced along that line from ear to ear across the top of their head. Depending on the size of your hands and the client's head, your fingers may be in different positions from the graphic. Remember that it is about intent and not about the exact placement of the fingertips. The practitioner will hold this position until the work feels complete. The process usually takes a few minutes. When complete, lift your hands and move to the self-love infusion step.

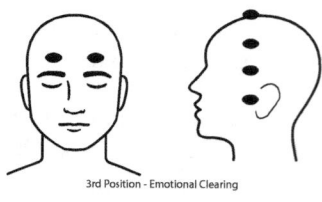

3rd Position - Emotional Clearing

Step 4: Self-Love Infusion

Move to the side of the table. Place your hands on or above the client's High Heart Portal, connecting deeply with their soul. Invite in the swirling, Divine masculine frequencies of white-gold. Allow those frequencies to blend and permeate High Heart.

Next, invite in the swirling, Divine feminine frequencies of rose-gold. Allow those frequencies to permeate High Heart and blend with the white-gold frequencies.

Next, bring in the frequencies of pure, Divine gold. These are the frequencies of Source, the One. Allow these pure love frequencies to permeate High Heart and blend with the white-gold and rose-gold frequencies, creating a triangle—the trinity.

Connect the Seat of their Soul with High Heart. Ask their soul to show you their true self, their Divine Essence, a projection of pure, unconditional love. Invite them to accept and absorb this feeling of pure love. Knowing that this is who they really are!

Note: There are multiple hand positions to Step 4.

Self-Love Spiral Infusion

Move your position around to the head of the table. Place your right hand along the right temporal lobe of your client's head. Place your left hand above the client's physical heart. (Respectfully find a mutually acceptable, safe place for hand placement on female clients.) Invite their head and heart to connect, allowing heart to directly communicate with head, softening any mental resistance to deep self-love. Hold this position until the head and heart connection feels complete.

Next, reposition yourself on the client's right side near their torso. Position both hands to be on/or above their Heart Chakra (respectfully). Visualize filling the client's heart with white-gold light. Imagine rose-gold light added to the white-gold. Then invite pure-gold light as you visualize all frequencies of pure, Divine love flooding their heart. Allow those gold colors and pure love to blend and expand their heart, creating a bubble of those gold colors. You may see the sign of the trinity or perhaps even a Merkaba. Ask their heart to open to the frequency of pure love. Allow their heart to fill with this love, showering their earthly self and form with pure love. Invite them to connect all aspects of self to Soul, Oversoul, and Core Essence.

Ask that they honor themself as worthy of love, made of love, capable of fully loving and accepting love. Ask them to accept this gift of pure love from their soul, knowing that as their soul loves them deeply, they can love themselves. As their soul showers them with love, so do the souls of others around them. Allow their heart to be open to acceptance of the love from those other loving souls in their lives.

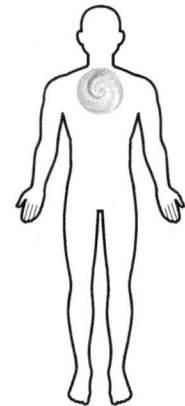

Moving in a clockwise spiral, bring your hands and the swirling bubble of white-, rose-, and pure-gold to their spleen, located at the bottom of the left rib cage. The spleen brings in life force energy (Chi). Visualize holding both front and back aspects of the spleen. Bring these frequencies and their Divine Essence into the spleen. Ask their spleen to open to the life force frequency of pure love. Allow the spleen to shift, bringing in the life force frequencies that resonate with this love energy. Let their spleen fill the meridians and the physical form with white-gold, rose-gold, and pure-gold frequencies. Let the spleen know that this higher form of life force is unlimited and abundant.

Continue the clockwise spiral pattern. Bring your hands and the swirling bubble of white-, rose-, and pure-gold to their Solar Plexus Chakra. Visualize the gold frequencies filling the torus of the Chakra, expanding and flowing through solar plexus, the seat of ego and sense of self. Invite their Solar Plexus Chakra to open to this Divine frequency and flow of pure love. Let it dissolve away the old, limited sense of self. Invite grace and forgiveness for self. Let the real power and loving self shine through like a beacon of light. Honor their true self as a child of the Divine. Visualize that child held and lovingly embraced by a Divine form, loved beyond all measure. Let them know they are valued and treasured by the Divine.

Moving in a clockwise spiral, bring your hands and the swirling bubble of white-, rose-, and pure-gold to their Throat Chakra.

Visualize the gold frequencies filling the torus of the Chakra, expanding and flowing into their throat. Invite their creative and communicative centers to open to that frequency of pure Divine love. Allow the inner voice to proclaim the depth of their self-love. Let it give voice to their value, their ability to love and to be love. Allow the throat to align with their soul and Divine will to express love in the world.

Continue rotating in a clockwise spiral as you bring your hands and the swirling bubble of white-, rose-, and pure-gold to their Sacral Chakra, connection to all relationships. Visualize the gold frequencies filling the torus of the Chakra, expanding and flowing through sacral. Invite sacral to fill with this frequency of pure Divine love. As their Sacral Chakra fills, ask that they allow these love frequencies to flow out all the loving cords that connect them to other hearts in their circle of relationships. Fill those connections with pure, unconditional love. Let the frequency dissolve all other cords, keeping only the loving, beneficial cords. Ask that they become aware of the love that returns along those connections. Ask that they expand their bubble of self-love, sending out love, noticing how the more self-love flows out, the greater the return flow of love back to them. Give gratitude for all the love they receive and deserve.

Moving in a clockwise spiral, bring your hands and the swirling bubble of white-, rose-, and pure-gold to their Brow Chakra, the seat of intuition and higher consciousness. Visualize the gold frequencies filling the torus of the Chakra, expanding and flowing into their Brow Chakra. Invite their brow to open to the frequency and flow of Divine love. Let that Divine love purify their higher thought processes and intuition. Bring awareness to the connection with all of humanity. Invite them to feel their resonance with the collective love of the planet.

As the flow continues moving in a clockwise spiral, bring your hands and the swirling bubble of white-, rose-, and pure-gold to their Root Chakra. Visualize the gold frequencies filling the torus of the Chakra, expanding and flowing into their root. Fuse the white-gold, rose-gold and pure-gold into their Root Chakra, allowing it to expand and flow with the pure love energy. Invite generosity to self into their root. Recognize that they are enough and have all they need. Invite their Root Chakra to connect deeply into the Pure Timeless Earth, being aware of the safety of the earth, sensing their soul's connection to the earth. Ask their soul to communicate its intent and strong purpose to be here, now on this planet.

Expanding the clockwise spiral, bring your hands and the swirling bubble of white-, rose-, and pure-gold to their Crown Chakra, the connection to the Divine. Visualize the gold frequencies filling the torus of the Chakra, expanding and flowing into the crown. Invite self-love to expand, feeling it resonate with the pure love of the Divine. Ask them to become aware how the Divine responds and sends back more love than imaginable. Invite them to allow, accept, and become one with the love that flows from the Divine.

Moving in a clockwise spiral, lower your hands and visualize the swirling bubble of white-, rose-, and pure-gold Divine love moving down to their Earth Star Chakra about 18 inches below the feet. Visualize the gold frequencies filling the torus of the Chakra, expanding and flowing into their Earth Star Chakra. Allow this Divine frequency to open and purify Earth Star, clearing ancestral and genetic interferences. Let this energy connect deeply into the Pure Timeless Earth. Invite them to sense this connection with the Divine form of mother earth. Feel her unconditional love. Ask that they know they are so worthy of this love.

Moving in a clockwise spiral, move your hands and the swirling bubble of white-, rose-, and pure-gold Divine love to their Gateway Chakra, several inches above the head. Visualize the gold frequencies filling the torus of the Chakra, expanding and opening this gateway. Invite the Gateway Chakra to expand as it fills with this pure frequency, clearing the connections to their soul, allowing soul to more fully express. Invite awareness that as soul becomes more pronounced, they are pure love incarnated.

Raise your hands and visualize the swirling bubble of white-, rose-, and pure-gold Divine love move to their Soul Star Chakra about 18 inches above the head. Visualize the gold frequencies filling the torus of the Chakra, expanding and flowing into their Soul Star Chakra. Invite awareness of the pure love of the Divine flowing through their soul and the entire body. Allow soul and body to merge as they become this Divine love.

Let the swirling bubble of white-, rose-, and pure-gold Divine love expand, connecting between Soul Star and Earth Star Chakras. Sense the creation of a möbius coil between them as this Divine frequency purifies their energy body and soul. You may sense the presence of unicorns or other guides as they are enveloped in this glowing bubble of love energy. Allow this bubble of Divine love to purify all aspects of the physical body, every cell, and the DNA within each cell.

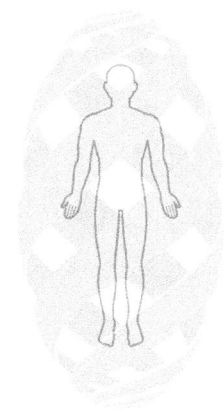

Let the swirling bubble of white-, rose-, and pure-gold Divine love expand into all the outer grid structures, hologram, and their matrix.

Invite in the 12 Rays of Light to reinforce the self-love bubble and let it resonate with the highest frequencies of the Rays available for the client today.

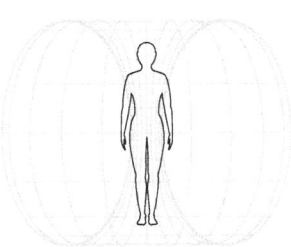

Ask the client to hold in their heart the profound connection to the Divine and the deep capacity for self-love that they have experienced.

Let them soak in these frequencies for a period of time to fully embrace all the shifts.

Step 5: Completion
As a final step, the practitioner visualizes streamers of gossamer threads woven and infused with iridescent diamonds, swirling around and creating a three-inch-thick cocoon of energy encasing the client. This protects and holds the energy, allowing time to integrate and assimilate the gifts of the session. Give gratitude to the many guides that have worked with you today.

Chapter Fourteen

Deeper Understanding,
Embodying Your Energetic Makeup

This segment of the workshop was designed to bring greater understanding of our energetic construct and systems. While it is important to understand these systems intellectually, we believe it is even more important to be able to self-sense our energetic systems. If we can understand and sense our energetic systems, then we will be more able to regulate them. Deeper understanding is also important to being able to feel at home with ourselves and to truly embody our energetic self and spiritual essence.

Let's begin to explore the Chakras and levels of the human energy fields. We will review some of the concepts that are in the earlier chapters of this book, then add more information about the conscious and unconscious aspects of the Chakras. The unconscious aspects are not consistently discussed in many books on Chakras, so this can be new information to some. The following table is a comparison to the difference in function of conscious and unconscious aspects of the Chakras.

	The conscious self	The unconscious self
Ruled by:	Laws of physical universe	Limitlessness of alternative realities
Regulates:	Our day-to-day realities	Our extended realities
Manifested by:	Following common-place procedures	Connecting to spiritual/cross-dimensional beings and energies
Contains:	Information about our current life, imprints from this life's decisions, needs, and experiences	Information about our past lives, imprints from past or alternative decisions, needs, and life experiences
Heals by:	Allowing us to interface with the tangible world; helping us "do it differently"	Allowing the intangible world to change reality for us

We move into exploration of the idea of the center point of the Chakras. Accessing the center point is a gateway to the quantum world and a pathway to a much deeper experience of the power of each Chakra. Some of the key things to know about the center point are:

- The center point of the Chakra system is the access point of "Pure Potential."
- There does not seem to BE form there, but it is the place where all things are pulled INTO form. In a sense it is the paradoxical point of both "nothing" and "everything."
- The center points run through the central column or channel of the Chakra system.
- It is the access point to the "zero point field."
- This center point is a "neutral" point, then it becomes activated when we call in the next expression of our highest light.

We now invite you on guided imagery journeys to experience the center or zero points of a couple of your Chakras. The Heart Chakra and 10th Chakra will be the Chakras to experience as they are both important and have contrasting characteristics. Take a minute to calm, center, and connect deep into Source and the Pure Timeless Earth. Hold your hands over your Heart Chakra, sensing into the energy of the conscious and unconscious aspects of this Chakra. After you spend some time tuning in and noticing these different aspects of the Heart Chakra, we invite you deeper into the center point of this Chakra. Explore the vastness of the zero point and the galaxy of energy and potential at that center point. Stay here a few minutes to experience the frequency.

After you have experienced your Heart Chakra, we invite you on a similar exploration of the 10th/Earth Star Chakra. Again, take a minute to calm, center, and reconnect with Source and the Pure Timeless Earth. Place the palms of your hands facing beyond your feet, and through intent, connect with your 10th Chakra. Begin to sense the energy of this Chakra and tune into the conscious as well as the unconscious aspects. Next, go a bit deeper with your awareness into the very center point of your 10th/Earth Star Chakra. Explore the vastness of the zero point, noticing the galaxy of energy and the pure potential of this energy. Stay with the sensations for a few minutes and notice the frequency.

We invite you to take a few moments to journal your experiences.

Self-Referencing and Other-Referencing

The next part of a deeper dive explores the concept of self-referencing versus other-referencing. These are ways of processing energetic information. One way is not better than the other, they are just different perspectives. This is an important area of exploration for the understanding of how we sense the world and create our reality. We all have some level of skills in both areas of referencing; however, generally one way is preferred or more strongly developed. Awareness of your preferences helps to regulate incoming information and allows one to create a better balance and stability of one's energy system. If we can learn and develop strength of both self- and other-referencing, it can enhance our ability to become more embodied.

Self-referencing is a form of self-tracking and self-awareness. Those who have strongly developed this sense tend to be better grounded and are more aware of themselves. They are more aware of how their personal space and energy are functioning, the size of their energy fields, and status of their Chakras. Someone who is strong at self-referencing is more able to notice subtle body clues (physical and emotional) such as tension in parts of their body in reaction to others or the environment. They are more able to energetically discern what is "me" versus what is "others."

Other-referencing is a form of external tracking and awareness of the energetic states of others around us. It helps us understand others more easily. Those that have highly developed this skill tend to live in their own upper Chakras and are less grounded. They have a heightened awareness of others. They are more aware of the space around them in relation to how others affect their own personal space. Those that have a more developed sense of other-referencing are aware of the subtle body and emotional clues in people around them. They are quick to notice what is happening in others and may have difficulty differentiating themselves and others. What is happening to another may feel like it is happening to them.

Before we had participants participate in experiential exercises with referencing skills, we discussed some important aspects of intuitive listening and experiencing. Focusing on these intuitive experiencing skills helps us to understand deeper what we sense in the exercises. We ask and remind participants to remember this list as they work with a partner in the experiential exercises:

- Hold a high frequency, stay connected to Christ Consciousness/ Source.
- Connect into your Core Essence.
- Sharpen your Chakra senses and listen with ALL your energy body.
- Check in with your body and your mind. What are you noticing?
- Listen for differences between words and tones in self.
- Be comfortable with silence.
- Ask open-ended questions.
- Recognize and trust what you know at your core (inner wisdom).

The first experience was designed to explore self-referencing. This was done as a self-experiential. We encourage you to slow your reading of this section and experience this in the same way the participants did.

We begin by asking you to become centered and connect to Source and your Core Essence. Quiet yourself and tune in to your physical and energetic self. We invite you to bring both of your hands to your Root Chakra. Slowly ask yourself the following questions, allowing time to observe and be aware of how your whole system responds:

- How does this Chakra interact with your energy field?
- Is the unconscious aspect under or overactive?
- Can you sense the difference between the unconscious and the conscious?
- How does your energy field look and how does that relate to the Hara?
- Pull your Hara thin and experience what your Chakras and fields do.

Next, we ask that you move your hands to your Heart Chakra, again slowly asking the same questions and allowing time to observe. When complete with the Heart Chakra, we ask you to move your hands to your Crown Chakra, repeating the exercise at that Chakra.

Following this experiential, we encourage you to take a few minutes to jot down your own experience in your journal.

The next experiential was designed to explore other-referencing. This exercise is done in pairs. We encourage the reader to find a partner to practice this exercise.

After finding a partner, choose which of you will be in the sensing role and which will be in the neutral role. Partners sit next to each other or in front of each other in chairs. We again begin by asking you to center and connect to Source and your Core Essence, quieting yourselves and tuning in to your physical and energetic self. With permission, the partner sensing gently places their hands on or just off the body of the neutral partner's Sacral Chakra. We ask the sensing partner to read the following questions, allowing time to observe, sense, and be aware of both the partner's energy as well as their own:

- How does this Chakra interact with their energy field?
- Is the unconscious aspect under or overactive?

- Can you sense the difference between the unconscious and the conscious?
- How does their energy field look and how does that relate to the Hara?

Next, we have the sensing partner move their hands to the Solar Plexus Chakra, again slowly asking the same questions and allowing time to observe and sense. When complete with the Solar Plexus Chakra, we ask the sensing partner to move their hands to the Heart Chakra, repeating the exercise at that Chakra.

Following this half of the experiential, we ask that the partners switch roles and repeat the entire sequence. After both partners have had a chance to experience both roles, we encourage you to take a few minutes to journal about your experience.

Again, as a reminder, the more aware we are of our own energy system and how we regulate in our day-to-day lives helps create better balance and stability of one's energy system, thus supporting easier flow and more embodiment of your spiritual and human self.

Chapter Fifteen

Quantum Hara Upgrade

The Quantum Hara Upgrade protocol activates points in the Hara that allow for deeper embodiment of our sacred selves. As noted earlier, one of the significant focus points of this book's material is embodiment. In the months ahead of the workshop, as we prepared, we were tuned into the idea of embodiment and meditating on that concept. During these preparations our guides revealed to us four additional points in the Hara which were not in our awareness. The guides made us aware of these Hara points, which we termed the Quantum Hara Points. These points are not new or "discovered," they are merely points that have been dormant in recent times. The energy of the planet and human evolution has moved to a time where these points are now accessible to be activated. Activation of these points was shown to us in a series of downloads over the previous year.

The four points are as follows:

- The Incarnation Embodiment Point: Located between the 10th Chakra and the core of the earth. Helps us deepen and hold the embodiment of this incarnation's work.
- The Soul Access Point: Located between the High Heart Portal and the Heart Chakra. Allows greater expression of Soul's connection and purpose.
- The Soul Embodiment Point: Located between the 9th Charka and the 8th Chakra. Helps us deepen and hold the Soul's embodiment.
- The Oversoul Access Point: Located between Oversoul and the 9th Charka. Allows greater connection and expression of Oversoul to Soul.

Curiously, the Extradimensional Charging Sequence we have been teaching and using for years was originally given to us using the upper triangle location of the Soul Embodiment Point, which is located between the 8th and 9th Chakras. We could never explain why it would be between the Chakras and the guides suggested it wasn't important then, so we told people to use the 8th or 9th Chakra as the upper triangle connection point, as it was easier to explain. Now we understand. We were not yet ready to understand these elevated frequencies at the time.

This protocol uses two different color frequencies as part of the activation and upgrade. The first of these is the color chartreuse. During the development of this workshop, the color and frequency of chartreuse kept appearing in many situations with our team. This chartreuse frequency purifies, infuses, and amplifies healing. We have clearly been shown the importance of this frequency and need to incorporate it in these healing protocols.

The second color frequency is pearlescence. The frequency of pearlescence is one of the pure Rays of Light, known as the 10th Ray of Light. It is overseen by Lady and Master Andromeda. Its purpose is soul integration and carries the qualities of soul acceptance and soul merge at a planetary level. Given our focus on embodiment, it is not surprising that we were guided to incorporate this frequency. When we started using the pearlescence, we realized that our guides as well as the Knights Paladin and Magenta Warriors had been infused with this frequency. This pearlescent infusion softened how they present to us, as their frequency shifted up in octaves.

The experiential is done working in pairs at a treatment table. One participant takes on the role of practitioner, the other the role of client or recipient of the work. After the session is complete and time is taken for discussion and reflection, the participants reverse roles so that both have an opportunity to give and receive. If possible, we suggest that you find a partner to practice this experiential.

The purpose of this technique is to:

- Increase access to the client's Oversoul and Soul and awareness of the purpose and lessons of this incarnation.

- Deepen the embodiment of the client's soul and mission of this incarnation.
- Activate and integrate the new Quantum Hara Points.
- Clear the client's Hara through all dimensions.
- Create new extradimensional crystalline geometry through access to the Quantum Hara Points.
- Upgrade Hara and Lightbody to new possibilities.

Step 1: High Frequency Shift—Self/Practitioner
The first step of the session is High Frequency Shift (HFS) for the practitioner. This is done while holding the feet of the client. The HFS brings the practitioner to the optimum elevated frequency to be the conduit for the client. It also serves to entrain the client in that elevated frequency, beginning the process of healing.

Step 2: High Frequency Shift—Client
The next step is to perform the client version of the HFS, ensuring the client is also at an elevated frequency.

Step 3: Reconnecting to Pure Timeless Earth
It is important for this protocol that both the practitioner and client are deeply connected to the Pure Timeless Earth to assure the purity of connections and access to the highest frequencies available.

Move to the foot of the table, holding the feet of the client. Focusing on yourself, connect to Source. Then connect deep into the Pure Timeless Earth, connecting through your Core Crystal. Deeply tune into your crystal as you allow your crystal to merge with the crystalline structure of earth as well as the matrix of the earth. Sensing into your Hara, run the frequency of Pure Timeless Earth from the core of the planet up, through your Tan Tien, Soul Seat, and Point of Individuation. Feel your strong Hara.

Ask the guides to help bring the client's energy down into the core of the Pure Timeless Earth. Sensing their Core Crystal also merge with the matrix of the earth core. Let the client entrain with your high frequency.

Step 4: Activating the Incarnation Embodiment Point

The charging sequence now uses the Incarnation Embodiment Point and the Soul Embodiment Points. Prior to using these points, they need to be activated. The next steps activate three of the four new points. This work is done standing along the right side of the client's body.

Visualize the client's 10th/Earth Star Chakra about 18 inches below client's feet and their Core Crystal in the center of the earth.

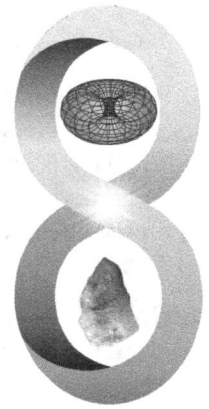

Visualize a möbius strip creating an infinity sign looping around their 10th Chakra and down around their Core Crystal. If it helps visualization, use your hands to trace the möbius strip.

Notice the point halfway between where the möbius strip crosses. That point is the Incarnation Embodiment Point.

Invite their Incarnation Embodiment Point within their Hara to activate and glow.

Allow that möbius strip to become a möbius coil, encircling both ends and further activating the crossing point where the Incarnation Embodiment Point exists.

Step 5: Activating the Soul Access Point

Continue standing alongside the client as the Soul Access Point is activated.

Visualize the client's Heart Chakra and High Heart Portal.

Visualize a möbius strip creating an infinity sign looping around High Heart Portal and down around their 4th/Heart Chakra.

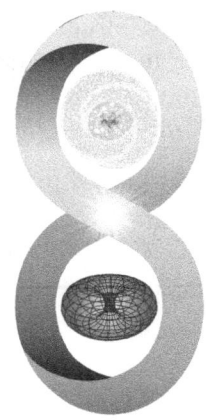

Notice the point halfway between where the möbius strip crosses. That point is the Soul Access Point.

Invite their Soul Access Point within their Hara to activate and glow.

Allow that möbius strip to become a möbius coil, encircling both ends and further activating the crossing point where the Soul Access Point exists.

Step 6: Activating the Soul Embodiment Point
Continue standing alongside the client as the Soul Embodiment Point is activated.

Visualize client's 9th/Soul Star Chakra about 18 inches above client's head and their 8th/Gateway Chakra.

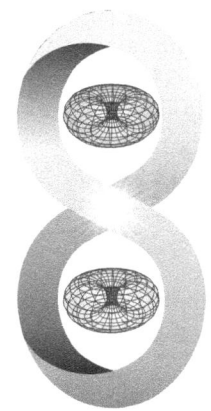

Visualize a möbius strip creating an infinity sign looping around 9th and down around the 8th.

Notice the point halfway between where the möbius strip crosses. That point is the Soul Embodiment Point.

Invite their Soul Embodiment Point within their Hara to activate and glow.

Allow that möbius strip to become a möbius coil, encircling both ends and further activating the crossing point where the Soul Embodiment Point exists.

Step 7: Activating the Möbius Connecting the Quantum Hara Points
As you continue standing alongside the client, visualize a möbius strip creating an infinity sign looping around the three Quantum Hara Points that were just activated in the client's Hara:

- Incarnation Embodiment Point
- Soul Access Point
- Soul Embodiment Point

Allow the möbius strip to strengthen, anchoring in the activation of the Quantum Hara Points.

Step 8: Extradimensional Charging Sequence

The Extradimensional Charging Sequence prepares the client for the deeper work of this protocol. The Extradimensional Charging Sequence opens and balances the energetic body while raising the frequency of the entire field. This version focuses the gridwork alignment into the newly activated Quantum Embodiment Points. Note: The upper point of the triangles anchors into the Soul Embodiment Point between 8th and 9th Chakras. The lower point of the triangles anchors into the Incarnation Embodiment Point between 10th Chakra and Core Crystal. This results in greater stabilization of the physical form to enhance the embodiment of our spiritual selves. The crystalline structure that's created supports the transmuting of non-beneficial energies and enhances the physical healing process.

This version of the Charging Sequence is highly supported by a group of guides as the practitioner uses their intent and visualization skills to direct energetic frequencies through the client. We begin by standing at the foot of the table and consciously inviting Archangel Zadkiel to the head of the table and the 12 masculine Knights Paladin to surround the client in their indigo frequency. Next, invite the Divine Wisdom to the foot of the table and the 12 feminine Magenta Warriors to create their ring of magenta around the client's energy field, encasing them in a bubble. Notice the frequencies of indigo and magenta interspersed with pearlescence flowing through the bubble.

As Zadkiel and the Knights Paladin are joined by Divine Wisdom and the Magenta Warriors, together they hold the outer edge of the client's field, as they tone their sacred ethereal sound. These 26 celestials will continue encasing the client and sounding throughout the protocol to support loosening and unwinding any fascial restrictions.

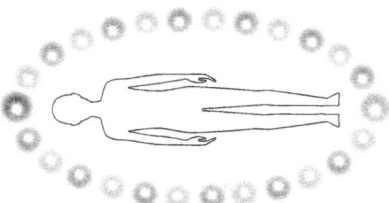

As the toning continues, place your hands on the bottom of the client's feet, one hand on each foot. At each position, the practitioner will intend that the body open, cleanse, and charge with the frequencies invoked. The guide's toning will clear and transmute in exactly the right way for this client in this moment.

You will focus on the creation of the triangles and the energetic connections from your hands through all levels of the client's being. Hold each hand position for at least a minute or longer, moving when that section of the body feels cleared and charged.

There are ten hand positions in the Extradimensional Charging Sequence listed below and shown in the illustration.

Charging Steps
The following are the hand positions:

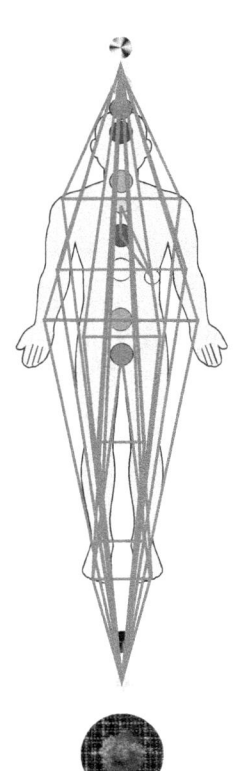

- Solar plexus reflex points of feet—creating triangles up to the Soul Embodiment Point and down to the Incarnation Embodiment Point.

- Same position, now connect to the Root Chakra and the Incarnation Embodiment Point.

- Both ankles—creating triangles up to the Soul Embodiment Point and down to the Incarnation Embodiment Point.

- Both knees—creating triangles up to the Soul Embodiment Point and down to the Incarnation Embodiment Point.

- Both hips—creating triangles up to the Soul Embodiment Point and down to the Incarnation Embodiment Point.

- Both wrists—creating triangles up to the Soul Embodiment Point and down to the Incarnation Embodiment Point.

- Both elbows—creating triangles up to the Soul Embodiment Point and down to the Incarnation Embodiment Point.
- Hands on the spleen and thymus, mentally connect to the Heart Chakra, creating a triangle of the three points (spleen/thymus/Heart Chakra).
- Both shoulders—creating triangles up to the Soul Embodiment Point and down to the Incarnation Embodiment Point.

Move to the head of the table. In the final position, you will place your right middle finger on the client's Brow Chakra. Position your left middle finger on their Zeal Chakra (at center indent point on occipital ridge). Position both thumbs on their Crown Chakra.

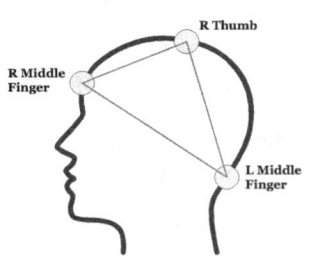

Visualize a triangle connecting these three points, activating the head centers (Brow Chakra/Zeal Chakra/Crown Chakra).

Step 9: Activating the Oversoul Access Point
Move to standing alongside the client as the Oversoul Access Point is activated.

Visualize the client's Oversoul and their 9th/Soul Star Chakra.

Visualize a möbius strip creating an infinity sign looping around their Oversoul and down around their 9th Chakra.

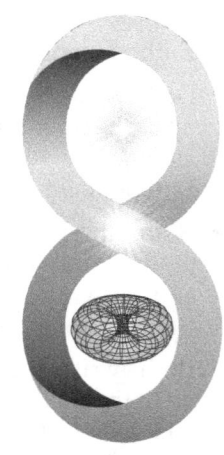

Notice the point halfway between where the möbius strip crosses. This is the Oversoul Access Point.

Allow that Oversoul Access Point within their Hara to activate and glow.

Allow the möbius strip to become a möbius coil, encircling both ends and further activating the crossing point where the Oversoul Access Point exists.

Step 10: Activating the Möbius Connecting the Quantum Hara Points

Check the activation of the other Quantum Hara Points previously activated.

Focus your attention on the activation of the client's Hara points, checking and reinforcing their activation.

- Incarnation Embodiment Point
- Soul Access Point
- Soul Embodiment Point

Step 11: Weaving the Quantum Hara Points

As you continue to stand at the right side of the table, bring your focus into the center of the client's Hara. Begin by asking the client's Hara to expand, widening to the optimum size for this moment.

Start by connecting through intent and reaching your hand to access the client's Oversoul Access Point above their head (visualizing it between their 9th Chakra and Source way above). Begin to weave a möbius strip down to the Soul Embodiment Point just above their head. Loop down and around their Soul Access Point at the upper chest. Continue to flow the möbius strip down to their Incarnation Embodiment Point way beyond their feet. Loop around and weave back up, creating a three looped strip, as shown in the figure.

This activates the notes within Hara, creating an opening in their Soul Seat.

Invite widening of the client's Hara to accommodate the greater energy of this expansion and activation.

Step 12: Clearing the Hara
Invite the guides to clear the client's activated Hara. The guides will be doing this work. You may witness or assist as they reach into the base of the client's Hara at their Core Crystal with their long etheric fingers. The guides will use color and frequency to clear, transmute, and purify the Hara. They slowly raise their fingers, combing through the Hara from base to top. You may sense things being removed, cleared, transmuted, and purified as the work progresses. The guides will make three passes from bottom to top. Each pass uses the perfect color and frequency to purify.

When the guides complete the clearing, they will infuse the Hara with chartreuse frequency from the core of the Pure Timeless Earth, through the client's Core Crystal, and up through the entire Hara. It may seem to come in like flames of chartreuse as it fills and infuses the chartreuse frequency to amplify the strength of the Hara.

Step 13: Remapping the Lightbody to the Upgraded Hara
Move up to the top of the treatment table. You will be working with the guides to remap the client's Lightbody. The guides will give you filters to recalibrate and integrate their Lightbody. Start high above the client's head at the outer edges of their grids and fields, asking that their Lightbody be recalibrated and integrated with the upgraded Hara.

Imagine holding a large hoop as the filter. Slowly pull the filter down the table, remapping as you go with the filters provided by the guides, integrating the Lightbody from top to bottom. After the first pass, return to the top of the table as the guides give you another filter. It typically takes three passes to complete the remapping. Stay at the bottom of the table after the third and final pass.

Step 14: Infusing Pearlescent Frequency Through the System
Stand at the foot of the table and hold the bottom of the client's feet. Visualize the client's earth crystal and invite the color and frequency of pearlescence into their Core Crystal, infusing it with the pearlescent frequency. When the crystal is fully infused, bring your awareness to their Hara, beginning to infuse the Hara with the pearlescent frequency and color. As you continue to hold the client's feet, slowly invite the pearlescence color and frequency up the Hara, coating the inside and outside of Hara. Allow the pearlescence to begin soothing, stabilizing, and flowing into all dimensions of their being as it calms and supports the new Hara structure. Continue to invite a flow of the pearlescence up their entire Hara all the way to Oversoul.

Step 15: Finalization

As a final step, the practitioner visualizes streamers of gossamer threads woven and infused with iridescent diamonds, swirling around and creating a three-inch-thick cocoon of energy encasing the client. This protects and holds the energy, allowing time to integrate and assimilate the gifts of the session.

Give gratitude to the many guides that have worked with us today.

Lastly, ground your client. Disconnect energetically and honor this beautiful soul that you have had the privilege to work with.

Chapter Sixteen

Evening Play Experientials

Experiencing Self and Others: Boundaries Work and Deeper Energetic Understanding

This boundary exercise is intended to allow participants to become more aware of their own energy system and also a chance to become aware and explore the energy system of another. This workshop included people with a variety of backgrounds and energy awareness, so we wanted to start with the basics. We gave participants a brief overview of the seven major Chakras and associated fields or aura. Readers have been given this information in the previous chapters of this book.

The first level of exploration was with self. Participants were voice-guided through a sensory experience touring each of their Chakras and each of the layers of the field. They were invited to journal what they sensed. After a break, they worked in pairs and were guided through a sensory exercise where they took turns sensing each other's energy fields and sharing their experience with their partner.

We additionally had participants come together in triads to explore sensing interactions with more than one person. This gave the participants an opportunity to share with another what they were sensing. One person would stand at a distance from the other two and observe the energy fields. This was a great experience for many participants as they don't generally receive feedback on how more than just one-on-one interactions can change the structure of an energy field. There were many "aha's" during this play time.

We encourage the reader to take a break and use their awareness to explore the current state of your Chakras and energy fields and journal if you wish. If you have a willing partner, you can do the exercise described with them.

We ended the evening experiential with a journey through the Chakras. Prior to this journey, we explored interweaving of the 8th through 12th Chakras.

Perspectives on the Multidimensional Interweaving of the Outer Grids

We are a complex interweaving of many multidimensional aspects of self. The outer and other multidimensional grids and fields intersect, interweave, interact, and communicate with the internal physical grids and networks such as fascia. The following is our current perspective on the interweaving of Chakras 8–12 and the outer grids and fields. We invited participants to experience and dive deeper into each of the higher-level Chakras using guided imagery exercises.

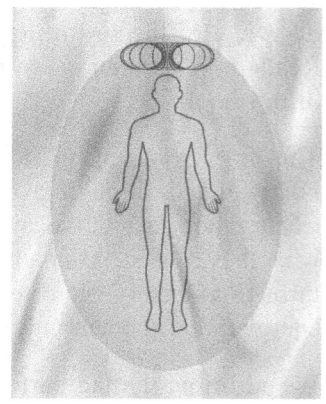

8th– Gateway Chakra; Iridescent silver: Higher purpose. The 8th Chakra holds information, allowing you to know and express your life purpose. Sense the presence of that information, allowing it to come forward as appropriate. 8th also facilitates connections to different dimensions and planes of existence. Sense into these connections. Some of these connections can be beneficial, some not so much. Notice any past and future lives, parallel or concurrent realities, and karmic patterns.

8th has a quantum correlation with the Soul Field Grid. Sense that if you can.

9th – Soul Star Chakra; Iridescent copper: Holds the projection of your soul's understanding of love and the lessons of love that you have planned for this incarnation.

How do you care for and connect with others? Can you access your soul's higher purpose? Do you believe you deserve love?

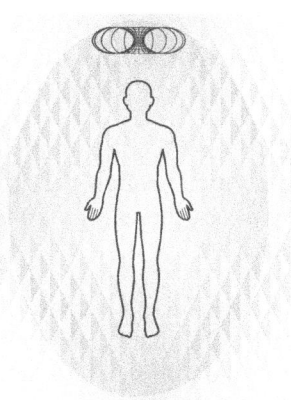

9th has a quantum correlation with the Incarnation Grid. Sense that if you can.

10th – Earth Star Chakra; Iridescent earth tones. 10th facilitates our interactions with the world and natural materials and the aspects of the natural world you connect with.

It holds ancestral lineages and the web of connections to all your incarnation timelines. It also holds DNA frequencies and epigenetic activations, both beneficial and non-beneficial.

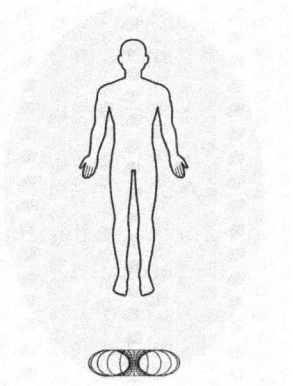

10th has a quantum correlation with the DNA Grid. Sense that if you can.

11th – Connective Chakra; Iridescent metallic blue. Our sense is that it is energetically intertwined with the fascial system, meridians, and Nadis. It connects through all dimensions of your being. As such, it is part of the internet of the body. Sense into these physical connections.

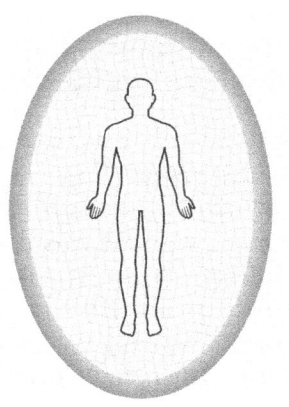

11th has a quantum correlation with the Fascia Grid. Sense that if you can.

12th – Golden Matrix Chakra; Iridescent gold. Connects all physical elements into the outer layers of the energetic shell that surrounds us, weaving together the physical and energetic.

Is your connection to all physical elements and the outer layers of the energetic field flowing and strong?

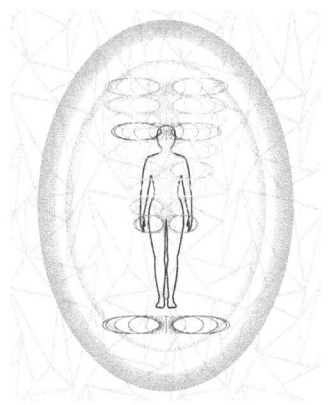

12th has a quantum correlation by weaving through the physical and all layers of the energy body. Sense that if you can.

There is also a quantum connection of the fascia that seems to be linked to the Tan Tien in the Haric dimension. Sense that if you can.

There is also a correlation between the Fascia Grid and in-body fascia:

- Your personal Core Crystal
- The Pure Timeless Earth's Core Crystal
- The crystalline matrix and grids of earth

Fascia quantumly connects to the earth grid system. Sense these connections if you can.

All 12 Chakras Experiencing and Healing Meditation

The following script was used as a guided meditation to sense deeper into our own Chakra system. We suggest you slowly read this and take time to ponder each part. Another possible way to experience this would be to record yourself voicing this as a guided meditation. Then play it back as you are in a more meditative state.

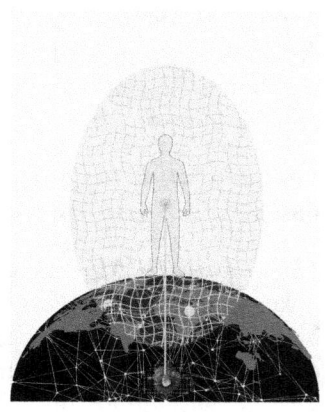

Take a few deep breaths. Connect to Source, connect deep into the Pure Timeless Earth, connect to your Core Crystal. Allow your crystal to merge with the crystalline structure as well as the matrix of the earth. Feel your Hara, invite the energy to flow from the core of the earth up, through Tan Tien, Soul Seat, Point of Individuation, and out to Source above and woven into the web of all creation. Feel your strong Hara as you deeply connect to the Pure Timeless Earth's Core Essence.

Bringing your awareness to your 10th/Earth Star Chakra, sense, experience, and envision liquid golden trinity light here. Sense the iridescent earth tones blended with the white-gold, rose-gold, and pure-gold trinity frequencies. Feel a sense within you to embody and have the willingness to accept the lineage you came onto the planet to support. Visualize the torus of your 10th. Sense as it flows, creating balance, stability, and vibrancy within the Chakra. As your 10th Chakra expands, drop into the zero point, a vibrant swirling galaxy of iridescent earth tones. See and sense that beautiful vortex from which everything emanates. Invite the full embodiment of this lifetime and the perfection of your soul's journey. See all your history and family lineage as a fabric woven just for you. Keep your focus here until you sense a full expansion and lighting up of your 10th/Earth Star Chakra.

Move your awareness and begin to flow the frequencies of your 10th Chakra up through the Central Channel to your 1st/Root Chakra. Bring more notice to the white-gold, honor the masculine aspect of self, and see the iridescent earth tones of 10th blend with the iridescent red of 1st. Feel the charging. Visualize the torus of Root Chakra expand and become more vibrant. Sense it flow and create balance, stability, and vibrancy within the Chakra. Notice who you are in the present moment as you allow for greater embodiment. As your 1st Chakra expands, drop into the zero point, a vibrant, swirling, iridescent red galaxy. Allow full access to this swirling galaxy of iridescent red infused with white-gold and iridescent earth tones as you invite deeper connection to your physical being.

Gently invite the frequencies to rise vertically up through your Central Channel to allow the energy to move up to your 2nd/Sacral Chakra. Notice the rose-gold here and honor the feminine aspects of self as the frequencies blend with the frequencies of iridescent earth tones, iridescent red, and the iridescent orange of sacral. Feel your Sacral Chakra expand with the vibrant colors of 10th and 1st. Let the frequencies dissolve all cords, keeping only the loving, heart-connected cords. Visualize the torus of your Sacral Chakra expand and become more vibrant. Sense it flow and create balance, stability, and vibrancy within the Chakra. As your Sacral Chakra expands, drop into the zero point, a vibrant, swirling galaxy of iridescent orange. Allow full access to the swirling galaxy of iridescent orange infused with rose-gold, iridescent earth tones, and iridescent red as the sacral expands to deep self-love.

Gently invite the frequencies to continue to rise as the energy moves up to your 3rd/Solar Plexus Chakra. Sense the white-gold and honor the masculine. Notice the other iridescent frequencies as they blend with the iridescent yellow of the solar plexus. Invite full balance in all of your human relationships. Visualize your Solar Plexus Chakra expand and become more vibrant. Sense it flow and create balance, stability, and vibrancy. As this Chakra expands, drop into the zero point, connecting with a vibrant, swirling, iridescent yellow galaxy. Allow full access to the galaxy of iridescent yellow infused with white-gold, iridescent earth tones, iridescent red, and iridescent orange as your Solar Plexus Chakra expands to create a fully balanced, healthy ego.

Invite the frequencies to rise toward your 4th/Heart Chakra. Experience the frequency of the rose-gold, honor your feminine aspects, and sense as it flows with the iridescent emerald green of the Heart Chakra. Feel the blending with all the vibrant colors of all your lower Chakras. Honor yourself as worthy of love, made of love, capable of fully loving, and accepting love. Visualize the torus of your Heart Chakra expand and become more vibrant. Sense it flow and create balance, stability, and vibrancy within the Chakra. As your Heart Chakra expands, drop into the zero point, a vibrant swirling galaxy of iridescent emerald green. Allow full access to this galaxy of iridescent emerald green infused with rose-gold, iridescent earth tones, iridescent red, iridescent orange, and iridescent yellow as the Heart Chakra expands to embrace your soul's full wisdom.

As the energy of your 10th Chakra continues to flow upward through the Central Channel to your 5th/Throat Chakra, sense the white-gold, honoring the masculine as it blends with the iridescent blue. Here we invite the Divine masculine and feminine to create balance in living our Divinity on earth. Visualize your Throat Chakra expand and become more vibrant. Sense it flow and create balance, stability, and vibrancy. As this Chakra expands, drop into the zero point, connecting with the vibrant, swirling, iridescent blue galaxy. Invite full access to the swirling galaxy of iridescent blue infused with white-gold, iridescent earth tones, iridescent red, iridescent orange, iridescent yellow, and iridescent green as the Throat Chakra expands to embrace your soul's Divine journey on earth.

As you invite the energy of the 10th Chakra to continue to flow upward to 6th/Brow Chakra, notice the rose-gold, honor your feminine aspects, and sense the blending with iridescent indigo. Feel your brow charge and expand with iridescent earth tones and all the vibrant colors of all the lower Chakras. Here we overcome our challenges with grace and ease to reach higher levels of spiritual mastery.

Visualize the torus of your Brow Chakra, sense it flow and create balance, stability, and vibrancy within the Chakra. As your Brow Chakra expands, drop into the zero point, a vibrant, swirling galaxy of iridescent indigo. See and sense that beautiful vortex from which everything emanates. Sense the blending of iridescent indigo infused with rose-gold, iridescent earth tones, and all the vibrant iridescent colors of the lower Chakras as the Brow Chakra expands to trust Divine guidance and your soul's plan.

Continue the flow upward to your 7th/Crown Chakra, noticing the white-gold and honoring the masculine aspect of self. Sense the blending with iridescent violet. Here we are asked to believe that any experience in our life is perfect and in Divine order and allow full connection or reconnection with the Divine spark that you are. Visualize the torus of Crown Chakra expand and become more vibrant. Sense it flow and create balance, stability, and vibrancy within the Chakra. As your crown expands, drop into the zero point, a vibrant, swirling, iridescent violet galaxy. Allow full access to this galaxy of iridescent violet infused with white-gold, *iridescent earth tones, and all the vibrant colors of lower Chakras as the Crown Chakra expands to surrender and trust the Divine order of your soul.*

Bring the iridescent earth tones of the 10th Chakra upward to the 8th/Gateway Chakra. Sense the golden trinity and iridescent silver as it fills your 8th Chakra. From here, observe the many lives you have lived, finding a gift in each lesson and experience. Visualize your Gateway Chakra expand and become more vibrant. Sense it flow and create balance, stability, and vibrancy. As this Chakra expands, drop into the zero point, connecting with the vibrant, swirling, iridescent silver galaxy. Invite full access to the swirling galaxy of iridescent silver infused with golden trinity frequencies, iridescent earth tones, all the vibrant colors of 10th and the 1st through 7th Chakras. As the Gateway Chakra expands, feel your connection with Oversoul and see your soul's roadmap.

Invite the iridescent earth tones of your 10th Chakra to flow upward to the 9th/Soul Star Chakra. Sense the golden trinity (white-gold, rose-gold, pure-gold) frequencies as it blends with the iridescent copper of the 9th. Feel the knowing of your soul and observe your grand story with clarity. Visualize your Soul Star Chakra expand and become more vibrant. Sense it flow and create balance, stability, and vibrancy. Drop into the zero point, connecting with the vibrant, swirling, iridescent copper galaxy. Invite full access to this swirling galaxy of iridescent copper infused with the golden trinity, iridescent earth tones, iridescent red, iridescent orange, iridescent yellow, iridescent green, iridescent blue, iridescent indigo, iridescent violet, and iridescent silver charge and expand. See the perfection of the Divine plan that you helped write. Realize that you ARE a spark of the Divine! This is a window to your own pure soul, your Core Essence at its highest frequency.

Invite your 11th/Connective Chakra to weave down through the fields. The 12th/Golden Matrix Chakra holds a shell around all of your fields. Continue to allow integration and full embodiment of all aspects of self as the Divine Being of Light that you are, here and now. Watch as all the colors glow, fuse, and become brighter as the swirling galaxies of iridescent frequencies allow you access to the quantum fields of your existence through all space and time. Invite healing and full vibrancy multidimensionally.

Feel your vibrancy! Allow quantum waves and sacred sounds to permeate all layers of your fields and grids.

Notice the golden trinity, the energies of white-gold, rose-gold, pure-gold, and all the iridescent colors as they flow through your whole physical body. Feel it flow within the fascia throughout your whole body.

Sense it through your bones. Your muscles. Through all of your organs. Through all your tissue. Into every cell of your body.

Allow the frequencies to flow beyond the body into the earth grids and matrices. Fully connecting and interacting with the Pure Timeless Earth.

Embody all aspects of your soul wisdom and Divine self.

Feel the new template of your whole energy system as it is upgraded.

Feel yourself anchored deeply into the Pure Timeless Earth. Feel yourself held by the planet and ready to do your work in this time and space.

Take a few deep breaths. Feel yourself back in this place and time, grounded deep into your physical body, connected to Source above, embracing your Divine essence.

Chapter Seventeen

Our Soul's Deepest Longings: Exploring Generosity, Grace, and Gratitude as we Dance with the Fireflies

Our Soul's Deepest Longing

Your soul's deepest longing is to realize the brilliant, infinite fullness and depth of your soul.

Your soul longs for you to know who you are as the Divine Being of Light that you are. Full of generosity, grace, gratitude, awe, and wonder. As we wander through our 3D life, it is hard to remember who we really are. It is even harder to remember that everyone else we meet is also a Divine soul and not the limited human being that is present to the outer senses. We began this portion of our presentation as a reminder to look deeper into our makeup and origin.

A common perspective is that we are the body, and we have a soul that is somehow contained within the body. Our perspective is that perhaps the body is in the soul, as the soul is much more than the body. As souls we are the consciousness of love in its purest form. The soul is not just part of the universe, it is part of the multiverse. Remembering who we are is beautifully explained by Rumi in his quote: "You are not a drop in the ocean. You are the entire ocean in a drop."

Since we are a Divine Being of Light, full of generosity, grace, gratitude, awe and wonder, spending time in these frequencies helps us to awaken and remember. Feeling awe happens in the presence of something that feels bigger than ourselves. Awe invites us to observe creation more deeply and possibly revise our understanding of the world.

There is a common thread in awe and wonder: It is being deeply present. In these moments of deep presence, we stop. We cease to think. We cease to judge. We cease to label. We ARE that presence.

> *"Wonder is that feeling of amazement mingled with admiration that is caused by something beautiful and unexpected."*[4]

Awe and Wonder Experiential

This experiential used the following script we created as a guided meditation to explore awe and wonder. As with other guided meditations, we suggest you slowly read this and take time to ponder each part. Another possible way to experience this would be to record yourself voicing this as a guided meditation. Then play it back as you are in a more meditative state. We advocate journaling about your experience.

> *Recall a time in your life when you felt awe and wonder. A time when you were deeply present for an experience. Maybe it was a time in nature, or the experience of a great love when your heart just burst open. A time when you had that childlike wonder. Can you recall that time when you were very present? Or when you have found a location in your mind's eye that soothed and excited your soul?*
>
> *When you have that moment recalled or captured, allow the feeling and experience to move through your physical body, as if it can move from the tips of your toes and fingers all the way up through your torso and head. Allow it to settle deep into your cells. Where do you notice the sensations in your body? Allow this experience and memory of that moment in time to refine your mind and move you into an awareness of the beauty and grandeur of life. Recognize the capacity for your heart to expand into a state of tenderness, kindness, gentleness, warmth, and caring. Hold this vision and put it in a place where you can access it at any moment.*

---

4 Oxford University Press. (n.d.). Wonder. In *Oxford English Dictionary*. Retrieved March 28, 2025, from https://www.oed.com/dictionary/wonder_v?tab=factsheet#14252761.

We hope you were able to find and reexperience a moment of awe and wonder.

You can open your eyes and come back to this time and space.

We invite you to journal about this experience.

Following Your Soul's Journey

Most of us think of ourselves as defined by our story, forgetting that our story is filled with self-judgment and limited perceptions of the incidents of the story. All of the life experiences of the story have left an impression. The most memorable moments have a feeling of pleasure (coming from a place of love) or discomfort (coming from a place of fear). We forget that our current life is one we chose to experience before incarnating. Life experiences are neither "good" nor "bad," they just are. Our soul is experiencing this life from a place of limited human perspective. Rather than getting caught up in the energy of our story, it is best to make peace with our past so we can realize a better future. From our human perspective, it can be hard to fathom that the soul is learning various lessons about the many aspects of love. Instead of searching for the story of our soul, we should try to follow our soul and let soul be our guide.

Your soul is well-qualified to bestow wisdom and direction upon you by following the guidance of your past, present, and future selves. Your soul is always trying to get your attention to get you to follow its wisdom. Use your intuition to listen to your soul. Note what sparks enthusiasm for you to follow your soul. Pay attention to those moments of intense enjoyment and interest in your soul's journey.

Your soul is learning the many lessons of love and is attempting to teach you self-love. We learn self-love by practicing the following qualities and attributes to and for ourselves:

- Compassion and Acceptance
- Generosity
- Gratitude
- Grace
- Respect and Honor

- Empathy
- Understanding
- Forgiveness

Compassion and Acceptance means accepting the "failures" without punishing yourself or having self-judgment.[5] Appreciating that you are perfectly imperfect. Learning to silence the inner critic. Realizing that the "negative" thoughts and experiences do not define you, they grow you. Acknowledging your shortcomings whether they are truths or only perceptions. Self-compassion and self-acceptance grow into a capacity for self-love. It also means accepting all parts of our experience without discrediting any parts of our life.

Generosity is usually thought of in relation to how we treat others. It is through kindness, selflessness, and giving to others that we are being generous. Generosity is thought of as being an act to benefit others, but contrary to that belief, the act of generosity increases our well-being. When we practice generosity, it incites in us a feeling of pleasure, trust, and social connection. It has a ripple effect and can inspire more positive emotions (leading us to joy, awe, and gratitude). We don't need to limit generosity to others. Be generous with yourself as well. Think of it as creating a hospitable place for your soul. By being generous to yourself, we are being more welcoming to our soul.

Gratitude is the "readiness to show appreciation for and return kindness" to self and others.[6] It is the appreciation for all this life has presented to us. Gratitude amplifies the good we see in ourselves and others. Gratitude can get us back on track to peace, joy, and contentment. Our lives are based on relationships. "Gratitude *is the moral cement, the* all-purpose glue, *the emotional filling, that squeezes into the cracks between people, and solidifying these relationships."*[7]

---

5 Neff, K. D. (2003). The development and validation of a scale to measure self-compassion. *Self and Identity*, 2, 223-250.

6 Oxford University Press. Gratitude. In *Oxford English Dictionary*. Retrieved January 31, 2025, from www.oed.com/search/dictionary/?scope=Entries&q=gratitude.

7 Emmons, R. A. (2016). *The Little Book of Gratitude: Create a Life of Happiness and Wellbeing by Giving Thanks.* Gaia Books.

Grace is to give love, forgiveness, and acceptance to self and others. Grace is an action word. Practicing grace affords you the power to influence your environment positively and inspire others to do the same, in turn. Grace contradicts our need to be in control, teaches us to let go and allow. Grace opens us to receive, welcome, and allow the good to flow in.

Respect and Honor for self is the structure of decisions you make for yourself, how you allow others to treat you, and how you treat yourself. Take care of yourself and your environment. Your beliefs and values mirror your sense of self. Honoring self means having a high respect and great esteem for self without the trappings of pride. Honoring self means to keep an agreement with and sticking to your personal code of conduct.

Empathy is "the ability to understand and appreciate another person's feelings."[8] As we begin to allow a greater understanding and acceptance of oneself, it allows us to develop stronger relationships. This, in turn, supports greater compassion and the ability to hear and possibly understand another's point of view. When we have empathy, we can observe from our soul level and see how this journey is not only about ourselves, but all others.

Understanding is to interpret or view something in a particular way, perceiving the intended meaning. To look at a situation from many points of view and have a greater understanding of the experiences we are having is our soul's exploration. As we view the world from an understanding perspective, we can remember that all things happen for us, not to us.

Forgiveness is the conscious decision to let go of the emotions and judgment for the thoughts and actions we or others make. Acknowledging poor choices also provides the opportunity for learning. Know that as our soul embraces forgiveness of others and self, each moment is a new opportunity for demonstrating that learning.

---

8 Oxford University Press. (n.d.) Empathy. In *Oxford English Dictionary*. Retrieved January 31, 2025, from www.oed.com/search/dictionary/?scope=Entries&q=empathy.

Meditation on Feeling Gratitude, Grace, and Generosity Within Our Physical Being

The following script was created and used as a guided meditation to tune into the ideas of gratitude, grace, and generosity to self. We suggest you slowly read this and take time to ponder each part. Another possible way to experience this would be to record yourself voicing this as a guided meditation. Then play it back as you are in a more meditative state.

Tune into your physical body and notice what you feel. Visualize scanning your body from head to toes and fingers. Do you feel any areas of tension or unease? If so, breathe into those areas.

Relax your face starting from the top down, collapsing your jaw, letting your shoulders fall away from the ears. As you notice them drop, let them fall away just a little bit more.

Take an easy breath and relax. Relax your arms and allow them to fall where they may. Breathe in and out, allowing your arms to fully relax.

As you move down the body, feel your hips. Are they comfortable where you are? Do you need to breathe into your hips and relax your legs just a bit more? Breathe in and out as you begin to relax your hips and legs.

Allow the energy to move down your legs to your feet and out the bottom of the feet. Breathe in and out as your feet soften into the earth.

Invite the energy to travel deeper into the earth to connect you to the Pure Timeless Earth. Feel your connection to the Divine Core Essence of Mother Earth.

As we move into a place of recognizing the frequencies of the following words, sense the energy in your body, paying attention to what thoughts or feelings might come forward for you.

Read these words slowly and just stay curious as you explore!

- **Gratitude:** That readiness to show appreciation or return kindness.

Sense deeper. Where might gratitude be expressed within your body or mind at this moment? Can gratitude bring forward an emotion?

- **Grace:** The feeling of being courteous. Having compassion, kindness, and love. Grace is an expression where we can experience honor. Where does grace come forward in your body? Your mind? Can you sense a memory or experience of grace as an emotion?

- **Generosity:** A large capacity of kindness. Where does this come up in your body or mind? Can you sense a memory or experience? Can you bring forward an emotion?

As you think about grace, gratitude, and generosity, consider: Were these experiences or memories from giving to yourself? Or were these experiences or memories of times you have given grace, gratitude, and generosity to others?

Let's travel back through these three words and feel them in your body one more time. As you reread these words, contemplate a time when you have given grace, gratitude, and generosity to yourself physically, mentally, or emotionally.

1. Grace:

- When have you given goodwill to yourself?
- When have you been courteous to yourself, showing self-compassion and kindness?
- Where do you feel the frequency of grace for yourself within your body?
- Does grace come up as a memory?
- Does it feel deserved?
- What does the word self-grace evoke for you?
- Do you feel worthy of having grace shown to yourself?

2. Gratitude:

- Have you ever shown yourself appreciation?
- Can you accept kindness and have gratitude for yourself? Where does gratitude for yourself show up in your body?

- Does gratitude for yourself show up in your mind?
- What does the word self-gratitude evoke for you?
- Have you allowed openness and kindness to be received by self?
- How does it feel to allow openness and kindness for yourself?

3. Generosity:

- Have you shown generosity of spirit to self?
- Where does generosity show up in your body?
- Does generosity for yourself show up in your mind?
- What does the word self-generosity evoke for you?
- Have you allowed yourself to be generous to self?
- Do you feel worthy of this generosity?

Notice how the recognition of self-grace, gratitude, and generosity can shift you physically, emotionally, and mentally.

Take a few deep breaths. Allow yourself to feel grace, gratitude, and generosity resonate as pure love within your body. Recognize it as the light of your soul—embody these qualities! Let yourself experience the frequencies of pure love filling every aspect of your being.

Take a deep breath and allow yourself to come back into the awareness of the present moment. Take note of all the frequencies you have experienced in your physical body. Spend some time journaling what you noticed and any new awarenesses that came forward.

Dancing with the Fireflies

The metaphor of "dancing with the fireflies" came to us as we were preparing for this workshop. As the theme kept showing up, we slowly realized how multilayered it was. In the simplest of ways, fireflies bring us into moments of awe. Each of us fondly remember those moments in childhood where watching the evening fireflies drew us into awe, magic, and wonder. Hopefully we can be as easily drawn there as adults.

A firefly's light comes from bioluminescence. Bioluminescence is the name given to the visible light emission from living organisms. This "phenomenon is widely distributed among animal groups, especially in marine environments. On land it occurs in fungi, bacteria, and some groups of invertebrates, including insects." Bioluminescence derives from a chemical reaction in which excess energy is transformed into light energy with very little being lost as heat.[9]

Fireflies are a representation of energy. When you see a firefly, you are drawn to it, seemingly inviting you to stop whatever else you were doing or where you were going to follow this little light. Fireflies do not "give off" any heat, only light that flickers like a diamond light and illuminates the darkest of spaces. Fireflies get 100% of their light from within themselves. Nothing outside is needed to produce that light.

Perhaps we are drawn to the firefly light as we have similar properties within ourselves. Our bioluminescence is more subtle, using biophotons. Numerous researchers have documented the existence of biophotons. "Biophotons are photons (light particles) that are generated within the body."[10] Photons have no mass; they function to transmit and receive information within and between cells. Photons are the means to transmit quantum bits (qubits) of information. The DNA in our living cells can store and release photons, creating these biophotonic emissions. Scientists state that there is optical (biophotons) communication happening in our brain. This suggests there is a strong link between these photons and our consciousness.

In general, there is one biophoton per neuron per second, but human brains can convey more than a billion biophotons per second. Is it possible that the more light the brain can produce and communicate between neurons, the more conscious we are? Another exciting implication is that this suggests that spirit and consciousness are not limited to being in our bodies, as quantum entanglement shows that when entangled, both photons react as one, even if only one is affected.

---

9 Bioluminescence. (2025, March 13). In *Wikipedia*. https://en.wikipedia.org/wiki/Bioluminescence

10 Srinivasan, T. M. Biophotons as subtle energy carriers. *International Journal of Yoga*, 10(2), 57-58.

This field of study is still in the early stages. Research from the Rhine Bio Energy Lab has demonstrated that the flow of "energy," "prana," or "chi" can be manipulated, with established physical evidence that this energy or chi exists in the form of biophotons (Baumann, 2012). The consciousness-like coherent properties of the biphotonic field are closely related to what researchers simply call the "field" and ancients called Brahma, the Dao, and other names. The intelligence of the biophotonic field may indicate a pathway for us to communicate with the non-physical realms of mind, psyche, and consciousness. Perhaps this biophoton energy was being described in the following quote from Paramahansa Yogananda:

> *"When modern science discovers how to go deep into the subtle electromagnetic constitution of man, it will be able to correct almost any medical condition in ways that would seem almost miraculous today. In the future, healing will be affected more and more by use of various types of light rays. Light is what we are made of—not gross physical light, but the finer spiritualized light of prana, intelligent life energy. That light is the real essence of everything. This earth is not "earth" as you see it; it is light. But you cannot perceive that until you know the underlying astral world."* – Paramahansa Yogananda

During the preparation of this workshop, we were shown multiple books by unrelated authors that described a common theme: They described a matrix or web that covers the earth with countless nodes that interconnect. These points of connection seem to be individual souls all linked together. Within the matrix there are varying degrees of brightness. We are all fireflies lighting up the web. The amount of brightness is related to our level of embodiment, how much of our Divine essence we can express in our consciousness.

A Soul/Light Journey from Source to Embodiment (Experiential)

This experiential used the following script as a guided meditation to explore our soul's journey from the decision to incarnate to the embodiment on this planet. As with other guided meditations, we suggest you slowly read this and take time to ponder each part. Another possible way to experience this would be to record yourself voicing this as a guided meditation. Then play it back as you are in a more meditative state. We advocate journaling about your experience.

We are going to go on a little journey. We will be going back to "The One" and bring you forward and experience your embodiment.

Invite your mind to not have to figure anything out; the information will come into your energy field and body, however you are ready to receive it.

Let's have some fun!

Visualize yourself as your Core Essence before you incarnated in this lifetime. Oh, your soul is so ready to come here, to planet earth, once again to learn lessons

- *What are you going to learn? You are so excited that you will get the opportunity to come.*
- *How are you going to get ready to come to earth?*

Imagine or visualize a large movie screen in front of you. On that screen there will be an overview of what you get to come to earth school and experience in this life. See what you see!

- *Why am I coming to the earth this time?*
- *Who do I get to run into?*
- *Who do I get to work with to teach me lessons?*
- *Who do I get to share these experiences with?*
- *What is it going to be like coming to earth school this time? You are so excited!*
- *What is my purpose in this life? I am going to choose the family that will best support me for that purpose, for my learning.*

Notice that you will be given many points in your movie overview or preview. These "choice points" will invite you to find more grace and gratitude for yourself and for the other souls you will be experiencing this new journey with. Let this movie play out as a brief overview, like a movie trailer.

Feel the excitement of your soul as you watch. Recognize that somewhere in your essence you know exactly why you are coming to earth.

As the movie continues, you get to travel to the earth. As that little soul, you get to anchor your Hara to the earth. Sense as you anchor the intent of being on planet earth at this time as your Hara anchors into the earth plane.

Next, anchor into your 10th/Earth Star Chakra as you choose this family that is going to support you. Recognize that it may not always be easy, and yet it is what you contracted for with each of them. To support you in learning all the wonderful things as your soul is ready for this earth life.

Anchor into your Core Crystal, the intent to be solidly here on the earth.

Next, anchor your Vivaxis into the Pure Timeless Earth grid lines and matrices, exactly where it needs to be.

Now you are ready to come in. You are ready to embody your soul in this human form. Free will plays into this journey in this life, as in every life. You have all the memories and experiences of past, present, and future lives simultaneously wrapped up in this soul of yours, so that you have access to your information to best support you on the way.

Whether you are born into the family you will be living with or be adopted, trust that that is part of the plan, your plan. Trust that your parents and grandparents and siblings all play a role in this beautiful life you have chosen.

Notice now the recurring patterns in this life that you have experienced and get to experience. Those might be one of the lessons that you are here to learn, that you decided to contract for. You may have said, "I want to learn what it is like to be humble. I want to learn what it is like to have a body that isn't like anyone else's body. To love myself so deeply, no matter how I look." Maybe you chose a certain challenge or gift just for someone else to learn a lesson. How fun it is to be able to experience life with others.

As you move through life, you might get clues as to what your soul knows to help you be on task, on path, on your journey absolutely perfectly. Even those choices you make might shift your path, and that is perfect. Even making no choice could be part of the adventure.

For there is no mistake, beautiful one, for you are on task, you are in-purpose. You are your soul's journey. Embodiment really means, how do you move in life to be on purpose and be the luminary that you are?

Take a few deep breaths as we close out your journey to this incarnation. Feel yourself here, now, back in this space.

Take some time to write in your journal about what came forward for you and what your soul would like you to know about this adventure here at earth school. We invite you to stay out of your mind and not try to figure out or analyze the adventure, but drop into your heart and trust what is being asked to come forward. For it is there, in your beautiful heart, you will know the answers of your soul.

Soul Growth and Soul Contracts

We all strive to understand our soul's mission and the many contracts we have in this incarnation. It is best to let our souls lead us rather than trying to understand from our viewpoint using intellect. Our souls express a frequency that enables us to create the footprint or a reverberation on our experiences and how our life affects others. These experiences invite us to embody our physicality and lead us to live at a soul level. As we connect and meet with others in this life, let the soul lead. Some contracts are short, some are lifelong. Life is a balance of holding and letting go as the soul learns its lessons. Free will plays a role and can change the nature of contracts. Soul contracts can be many things, including the following:

- An earth school lesson plan that we chose. We make a general outline to learn about some aspects of love, for example: trust. We then experience situations of trust or broken trust to learn different aspects of that theme.

- We are here to experience contrast in this realm to grow our soul. We need the contrast in order to learn. We would not learn if we only saw things from one perspective. The contrast or duality is an inherent part of this earthly existence.

- It is a privilege and an honor for our soul to be here. Much channeled information has a similar theme: Earth school is difficult and only the bravest souls take on this journey. We are fortunate to have this privilege.

- It is what you have come to work out or heal on earth in this lifetime. Often the most difficult challenges are the key lessons that we are here to learn this time.

- We chose our soul family (whether biological or not). We chose our physical family and the supporting cast of souls that we will primarily work with this lifetime. We have probably, although not always, worked with these fellow souls on other lessons in other lifetimes.

- Soul contracts can move from lifetime to lifetime. Some contracts and learning experiences continue for many lifetimes until the lessons are learned.

Experiencing the gifts and challenges in contracts allows for further soul growth. How we experience life events depends on the clarity of our filters. We filter all our experiences through a lens of variable clarity. Clouding of the lens keeps us from seeing the soul's plan and orchestration of our lives. A cloudy lens will tend to distort our perception. That distortion leads to the belief that things are happening to us. When we believe that things are happening to us, we tend to blame, judge, and feel out of control.

If we can clear the lens, we will see that the soul, which is ourselves, is taking the lead. Things that happen are orchestrated for our own good and learning. They are happening "for us" rather than "to us." Even with the experiences that may seem terrible on the surface, the soul is unharmed. The more we move to the attitude of "for us," the more we can appreciate our soul and allow the filters to begin to clear.

As the lens clears, we can begin to realize that we are all the same. We are all souls here for different lessons and different experiences. We have probably all played both sides of the many roles at one time or another (warrior, victim, perpetrator, healer, royalty, and peasant). Remember that we had the privilege and bravery to choose this experience on earth. This beautiful reminder tells us that the soul is unharmed and we have the opportunity for growth and expansion— clearing old stories, energies, and stepping into being a source of Light for Gaia, the Pure Timeless Earth.

Chapter Eighteen

Souls Embodiment Healing

Building on the work of the previous chapter about our soul's deep longings, this protocol clears the way to realize those longings.

This experiential is done working in pairs at a treatment table. One participant takes on the role of practitioner, the other the role of client or recipient of the work. After the session is complete and time is taken for discussion and reflection, the participants reverse roles so that both have an opportunity to give and receive. If possible, we suggest that you find a partner to practice this experiential.

At the workshop, each participant was given an energetically cleared quartz crystal. While on the treatment table during the healing exchange, the crystal was placed on the client's Heart Chakra at the "soul remembering" step of the protocol. This crystal was then kept by the participant and utilized later in the evening intuitive sharing time.

The purpose of this technique is to:

- Invite realignment of any soul contracts, agreements, arrangements, and pacts to be upgraded to the highest frequency for the client's greatest soul growth.
- Fully embody, expand, and strengthen the truth of the client's earthly choices.
- Strengthen all soul contracts, agreements, arrangements, and pacts aligned with the client soul's purpose.
- Connect to Oversoul to support deeper knowing of truth, longing, and pure intent for this lifetime.

- Activate and strengthen the Quantum Hara Points for greater access to the client's soul longing and purpose (Oversoul Access/ Soul Embodiment/Soul Access/Incarnation Embodiment).

- Activate the biophotons and consolidate the whole upgraded energy system.

Step 1: High Frequency Shift: Self
The first step of the session is High Frequency Shift (HFS) for the practitioner. This is done while holding the feet of the client. The HFS brings the practitioner to the optimum elevated frequency to be the conduit for the client. It also serves to entrain the client in that elevated frequency, beginning the process of healing.

Step 2: High Frequency Shift: Client
The next step is to perform the client version of the HFS, ensuring the client is also at an elevated frequency.

Step 3: Clearing and Expanding the Energy System
From the foot of the treatment table, bring your attention to the client's 10th/Earth Star Chakra. Using your hands, above the body, begin to slowly spin a clockwise vortex of pure Divine golden light at their 10th Chakra. Invite the Comet Beings to blend and infuse the golden light deep into this Chakra. The first pass clears the physical body.

As you continue spinning the golden vortex clockwise, slowly move farther up and around the body to clear, open, expand, and prepare the energy system.

Let the golden vortex expand out to the width of the 12th level of the energy field.

Flow this golden vortex with the Comet Beings up farther beyond the 9th Chakra. When the first pass is completed, move back below their feet to the 10th Chakra.

Make five passes to clear each of the energy bodies:

- Physical
- Emotional
- Mental

- Spiritual
- Holographic Bodies

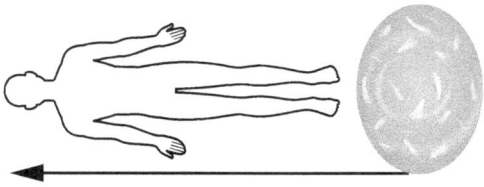

Step 4: Soul Contract Realignment

Move to the right side of the treatment table, placing one hand on the client's Heart Chakra and the other on their High Heart Portal at the Seat of their Soul. Allow your breath to come into sync with the client's breath and invite connection with their Soul Field and with their Oversoul. As you continue to hold Heart Chakra and High Heart Portal, we invite soul contract realignment. State the following requests out loud so the client can hear them:

- We ask the guides to help the client to retrieve any aspects of their soul they may have given away for someone else to hold. Pause and give this time to complete. This may take a few minutes.

- We ask the client to release any aspect of the souls of others they might be holding. Pause and give this time to complete. This may take a few minutes. (This often feels more important than the first statement.)

- We ask that all contracts that are no longer in their highest good at this time be dissolved and released. Pause and give this time to complete.

- We ask that only loving contracts or agreements be allowed to flow in all directions. Pause and give this time to complete.

Step 5: Soul Misinformation Clearing

Come to the head of the table and reach up above the client's head, connecting to their Oversoul.

The guides will give you a specific tool or mechanism to move through their Hara to clear out any misinformation or misguidance around the client's soul purpose. This feels more like a tool rather than the filters we have used in the past. Many experience this as a spinning disk or some other clearing and polishing tool. This clears out information that is not the client's truth.

As you gently assist, the guides slowly pull this rotating mechanism down through the Hara, inviting purification and releasing.

As you support moving this spinning tool down the body through the Hara, it may pause as some things get loosened that may be embedded. Those are things that are not in alignment with the client's soul's purpose or longing. Hold as you allow those energies to move out.

You may sense it moving through the exterior as well as the interior of their Hara.

Continue to move down the body as well as all the layers of the earth grids to the client's Core Crystal within the Pure Timeless Earth.

When you reach their Core Crystal, pause and release the tool. The guides will then give you a new mechanism to use going back up the Hara. Slowly reverse and draw this mechanism up the Hara from their Core Crystal, through the body, and out the top of the head and beyond the 9th Chakra up to Oversoul.

Repeat moving a mechanism/tools down and up the Hara two more times (three times total). You may sense that the tool shifts or a different mechanism is given for each pass.

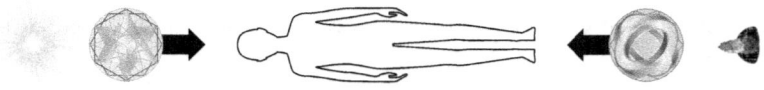

Step 6: Soul Intention
For the workshop, we had the practitioner place a cleared quartz crystal on the client's Heart Chakra. This was used later in the evening for intuitive play. (Placing the crystal is optional.)

Stand along the right side of the table, placing one hand on the client's Heart Chakra and the other hand on their High Heart Portal. Connect with the client's Oversoul, bringing awareness to what their Oversoul knows before incarnating; ask that they be shown their true and pure soul intent for this lifetime.

Pose in your mind's eye these questions as you are connected to the client's Oversoul. (Allow your client to come into alignment as they are ready to know the answers.) Pause with each question and give time for the response to settle in. Words or full understanding may not come for the client, but the energetic knowing may come forward. Allow that to be enough.

What is their soul's purpose? Invite them to ask their soul what brings them:

- Joy
- Awe
- Wonder
- Tranquility
- Passion
- Enthusiasm
- Gratitude for self

Step 7: Soul Re-remembering Activation with Crystalline Structure
Move to be above the client's head as you continue to hold that connection to Oversoul.

Pause here. The guides will give you a crystalline structure/pillar/cylinder with streams of lights to fully activate Divine "re-remembering" of their soul's purpose. We have experienced this as a large crystalline tube that encases the client. The crystal pillar or tube is filled with lights of shifting frequency. Practitioners will slowly guide this structure down along the line of the Hara. As the crystal structure comes down the Hara, pause at each of the Quantum Hara Points. The activation creates greater strength in remembering and embodying all aspects of the soul's purpose. (If the client is holding a crystal, hold your awareness of that crystal as you pause at each of the Quantum Hara Points to activate as the encoded information can be captured in the structure of the crystal.)

Stop first at:

- Oversoul Access Point: Between Oversoul and 9th Chakra
- Soul Embodiment Point: Between 9th and 8th Chakras
- Soul Access Point: Between the High Heart Portal and the Heart Chakra
- Incarnation Embodiment Point: Between 10th Chakra and the client's Core Crystal

Stepping to the right side of the client, continue to hold the crystalline structure/pillar in your awareness.

Place one hand on the client's right shoulder and one hand on their right thigh.

Allow the frequency of the crystalline light to continue flowing beyond the Incarnation Embodiment Point, reaching the client's Core Crystal within the Pure Timeless Earth. Invite a melding of their soul's purpose with their Core Crystal. This will support a deeper ability to be on earth and step into their purpose.

As you intentionally connect with the Core Essence of Mother Earth, ask the client to invite deeper embodiment of their soul's longing and purpose. Let it expand and strengthen. Invite a continued flow and melding with the Pure Timeless Earth's core.

As the frequencies meld, there is an igniting, activation, and alignment with all the gridlines and matrices of the earth to fully embody the client's soul's purpose as it weaves with the Pure Timeless Earth.

Hold here as you sense awe and wonder within the client, as they fully embody their soul's deepest longing.

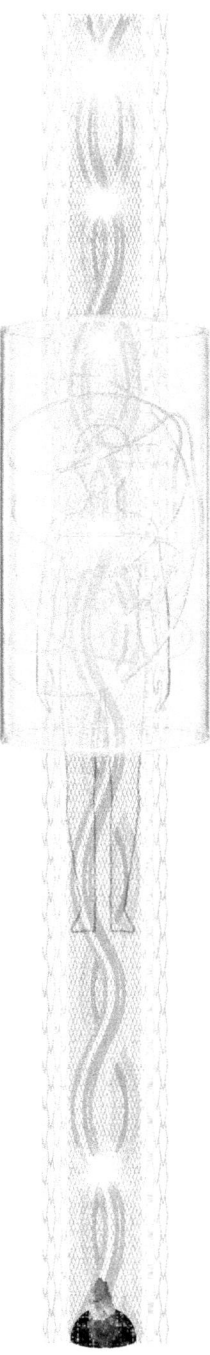

Step 8: Biophoton Activation Through the Brain
Move to the head of the table and gently hold (cup) one hand on each side of the client's head just above the ears. Invite activation of the biophotons through the brain. You may sense a gentle pulsing between your hands during activation. Witness the biophotons illuminating and activating. As you hold, visualize a link up to the client's Soul Field Grid, creating greater alignment with their soul's wisdom. Hold and allow as this activation occurs. This may take several minutes.

Step 9: Biophoton Activation: Firefly Spark
Continue to hold your right hand just above the client's right ear and move your left hand to the client's heart, allowing heart and head to connect. Sense a pulsing between their head and heart as a greater flow creates balance between these points.

Invite the fireflies to be the spark of remembering for all the biophotons to activate and to hold activation throughout their whole body. Notice as all the cells light up. Sense into the structures and matrices within their body and beyond the body. Invite the biophotons to come into resonance with their soul's purpose, lighting up, and bringing soul cohesion to the whole field.

Step 10: Biophoton Activation: Quantum Hara Points and Heart
Continue to hold your right hand just above the client's right ear and your left hand at the client's heart as we invite full flow of the biophotons and anchoring into each of the Quantum Hara Points and connection into the client's heart. Hold here until you get a sense of full flow, activation, and illumination through the heart, the Quantum Hara Points, and every cell of their body.

- Oversoul Access Point: Between Oversoul and 9th Chakra
- Soul Embodiment Point: Between 9th and 8th Chakras
- Soul Access Point: Between the High Heart Portal and the Heart Chakra
- Incarnation Embodiment Point: Between 10th Chakra and client's Core Crystal

Step 11: Integration of the Entire System— Weaving with Möbius Coil

Move to the side of the table and using your hands, weave with a möbius strip from the 10th/Earth Star Chakra to 9th/Soul Star Chakra, passing through the Heart Chakra to strengthen and consolidate the entire energy system.

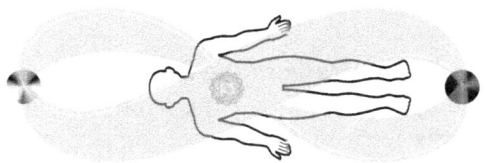

Trace this pattern with your hands several times until you sense the flow and the move-ment becomes a möbius coil enveloping the entire energy system. Allow time as your weaving becomes consolidated, strength-ened, and set. See figure to the right.

Step 12: Crystalline Star Anchoring

Standing along the right side of the table, hold your hands open and palms upward above the client. Visualize an eight-sided crystalline star in your hands. This crystalline star is a gift to anchor and support stability of remembrance of who they are and what their true purpose is, inviting them to remember that they are "in purpose" in every moment. It is the journey that is the purpose.

As you hold the star, it will expand and open into a billion stars, drifting into the client's field and down into each cell of their body. These billions of stars anchor into the body, the field, and the biophotons, creating pro-tection and stability. A reminder that all the new frequencies can be integrated into the whole energy system and grow stronger.

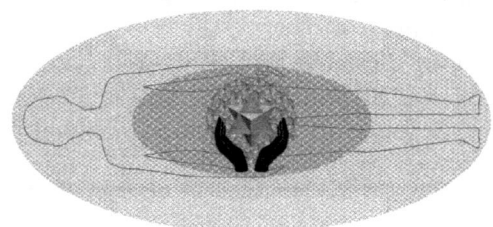

Step 13: Anchoring Physically to the Pure Timeless Earth

Move to the foot of the table. Place the palms of your hands on the soles of the client's feet. Visualize a plasma with rich, iridescent neon orange energy pouring from the palms of your hands. Allow the energy of the iridescent neon orange to come up from the Pure Timeless Earth, grounding through the Vivaxis, anchoring Hara, and flowing through your hands.

Allow it to flood up into every cell of the body, through all the bones, fascia, muscles, organs, and template of the body as well as all the fields. This will support these frequencies in grounding and anchoring to assist in strengthening the physical form.

Step 14: Finalization

Continue to hold the client's feet as you ask Archangel Raphael to bring in sparkling iridescent green light. This frequency flows through your hands to flood the bones, fascia, muscles, organs, and template of the body as well as all the fields to promote healing and finalization.

As a final step, the practitioner visualizes streamers of gossamer threads woven and infused with iridescent diamonds, swirling around and creating a three-inch-thick cocoon of energy encasing the client. This protects and holds the energy, allowing time to integrate and assimilate the gifts of the session.

Give gratitude to the many guides that have worked with you today.

Lastly, ground your client. Disconnect energetically and honor this beautiful soul that you have had the privilege to work with.

Chapter Nineteen

Quantum Linkup of Primary Cell Matrix

The Primary Cell Healing protocol was preceded by a description of the Primary Cell and a discussion of events that may cause distortion of the Primary Cell. Chapter 4 gives an overview of the Primary Cell.

A healthy Primary Cell resonates with the vibration of the universe to keep us in sync with our birth intentions. We think the primary interface is through the Incarnation Grid. The Primary Cell remains undamaged but can be hindered from reaching its full potential. Trauma affects the epigenetic expression of the Primary Cell.

Some events that contribute to clouding, disconnection, and distortions to the Primary Cell include:

- Traumatic life events—significant life traumas may induce fears, stress, judgment, guilt, etc.
- Trauma (past lives and present) can disrupt the ability to fully achieve our potential, affecting the Primary Cell.
- Transgenerational trauma and perceptions can undermine our sense of wholeness and damage, distort, and/or disconnect the Vibratory Grid Lines from the Spin Points and limit the ability of the acupuncture meridians and body to access energy.

These disconnects and distortions may be experienced or perceived as binding, occluding, or shielding the Primary Cell from healing energies.

Healing of the Primary Cell realigns it with the Incarnation Grid and Lightbody, reactivating the ability to achieve full potential. A fully activated Primary Cell remembers and begins to embody its Divine original blueprint in resonance with the vibration of the universe and the soul's birth intentions. Its remembered and embodied frequency expands into every level, realigning the entire Lightbody and all grids. Primary Cell healing brings this realignment down from Lightbody into all layers, restoring the ability to achieve full potential.

Primary Cell Self-Exploration (Group Guided Meditation)

The intent of this guided meditation was to allow Primary Cell to reach full potential in this moment. The following script was used as a guided meditation. We suggest you slowly read this and take time to ponder each part. Another possible way to experience this would be to record yourself voicing this as a guided meditation. Then play it back as you are in a more meditative state.

Invite the Iridescent Masters to clear your Incarnation Grid as they bring filters from above the 9th Chakra down past the 10th Chakra to realign your Incarnation Grid with your life's purpose and your work on this planet. As the Iridescent Masters very slowly pass the first of three filters from above your head to below your feet, you may sense things releasing and moving out. They bring a second filter and slowly move it from above your head to below your feet. Sense as there is more clearing and realigning of your Incarnation Grid. A third pass and final from above the 9th Chakra to below the 10th Chakra, recalibrating, realigning, and smoothing.

Next, bringing your hands in front of your physical heart, become aware of your Primary Cell somewhere in your body. Invite your Primary Cell to come into the palms of your hands. Visualize Primary Cell moving from wherever it came from in your body as it moves into your hands. Notice if there are any bindings or obstructions (maybe wrapped in tangles, bound, or locked in a chest). Allow your Primary Cell to free itself, to unbind, to unfurl, and melt any restrictions.

Now shower your Primary Cell with the light of your Core Essence and pure love from your heart; feel your love for your Primary Cell.

Next, invite in iridescent rainbow and pearlescent colors to shower down into your Primary Cell. Visualize this rainbow of colors as they interact with the spirals, the strands of your DNA. The rainbow and pearlescent frequencies light up your DNA, making any changes that are for your highest good at this time.

Notice how much clearer and brighter your Primary Cell is.

Now imagine a stream of energy that creates a möbius strip (figure eight) that wraps around the Primary Cell and up to the Incarnation Grid. See a flowing, weaving möbius strip of energy surrounding Primary Cell, connecting and interacting with your Incarnation Grid.

Then see another möbius strip going down, wrapping around Primary Cell and down to your 10th Chakra below your feet, anchoring Primary Cell into your Earth Star and the earth.

Those two möbius strips become a multifaceted möbius coil, crossing at the Primary Cell, linking you to the Pure Timeless Earth and to your Incarnation Grid. Hold as a full link-up occurs.

Next, bring your hands to your heart, inviting your newly revised and revived Primary Cell into your heart. Feel it blend and connect with the tissue and the fascia of your heart. With three deep breaths, breathe it in deeper so that all of the fascia of the heart is fully infused with the revised DNA of your Primary Cell.

Breathe that frequency into your upper chest, your back, and all of the upper torso, connecting all of the fascia with Primary Cell's energy. Then visualize connecting all the lower part of your torso, all the organs there and your lower back, as you breathe that energy into the fascia, the connective tissue of the lower torso.

Using your breath, breathe those frequencies into your head. Feel the fascia light up and rewire all cells and the neural pathways of the brain.

From your shoulders and chest, breathe it down each arm to your finger-tips, lighting up the fascia.

Breathe the activated frequency into the pelvic area and down each leg. Feeling the fascia expanded and free.

Feel your whole body energized. All the fascia has new informa-tion to support your realigned energy system, fully connecting the Primary Cell with your Incarnation Grid. Upgraded fascia is the primary gridwork for bringing this into the body, connecting it to every cell.

Be aware of how your Core Essence is at a higher frequency and elevated. Every cell in your body is lit up to this new higher frequency. Know that you can maintain this, you can come back to this. This is YOU!

When you feel ready, take a few deep breaths and bring yourself back to this space and time. Feel fully connected and grounded in your body.

We encourage you to put down the book at this time to reflect and take notes in your journal.

Quantum Link-up of Primary Cell Matrix Healing Protocol

The experiential is done working in pairs at a treatment table. One participant takes on the role of practitioner, the other the role of client or recipient of the work. After the session is complete and time is taken for discussion and reflection, the participants reverse roles so that both have an opportunity to give and receive. If possible, we suggest that you find a partner to practice this experiential.

The purpose of this technique is to:

- Release any bindings and constraints to the client's Primary Cell.

- Allow Primary Cell to release trauma and remember the pure Divine template aligned with the client's soul's plan for this incarnation.

- Realign Lightbody and the entire energetic system to be aligned with the client's soul's plan.

- Restore ability within the client to achieve and embody their Divine full potential.

• Reweave healed energy systems into the fabric of the earth grids, lifting the frequency of all humanity.

Step 1: High Frequency Shift: Self
The first step of the session is High Frequency Shift (HFS) for the practitioner. This is done while holding the feet of the client. The HFS brings the practitioner to the optimum elevated frequency to be the conduit for the client. It also serves to entrain the client in that elevated frequency, beginning the process of healing.

Step 2: High Frequency Shift: Client
The next step is to perform the client version of the HFS, ensuring the client is also at an elevated frequency.

Step 3: Charging Sequence
The Charging Sequence prepares the client for the deeper Primary Cell work. This version of the Charging Sequence brings in the firefly frequency to assist with the clearing and charging at each hand position.

Begin at the foot of the treatment table with your hands on the bottom of the client's feet. At each position, the intent of the practitioner will be that the body open, cleanse, and charge with the frequencies invoked. Hold each position for a minute or until it feels open and is flowing. Then move up the body to the next position as illustrated in the figure, inviting the firefly frequency throughout.

1. Hands on bottom of feet.
2. Both ankles.
3. Both knees.
4. Both hips.
5. Both wrists.
6. Both elbows.
7. Both shoulders.
8. Both sides of the head.

Step 4: Spiral Infusion of Trinity Gold and the Flight of the Fireflies
Move to the client's right side of the table. Hold your hands above the client's Heart Chakra and imagine a swirling bubble of love energy filled with white-gold, rose-gold, and pure-gold energy. Invite hundreds of fireflies to join and swirl with the gold frequencies in that bubble.

As the frequencies of the golden trinity and the fireflies swirl in your hands, invite the bubble into the client's Heart Chakra. Ask that they open their heart to the frequency of pure love and the joy and awe of the firefly energy. Allow their heart to fill with this love and high frequency energy. Ask that they honor self as worthy of love, made of love, capable of fully loving and accepting these gifts.

When the client's Heart Chakra is filled, move in a clockwise spiral, bringing the swirling bubble of golds, the fireflies, and your hands to their spleen, allowing time for the spleen to fill with this energy.

As each area is filled, continue to move in a clockwise spiral sequence, infusing with the trinity of gold and firefly frequencies as indicated in the figure.

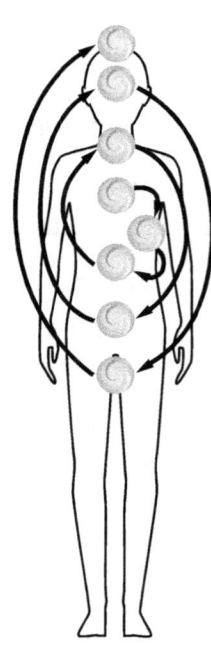

- Heart Chakra
- Spleen
- Solar Plexus Chakra
- Throat Chakra
- Sacral Chakra
- Brow Chakra
- Root Chakra
- Crown Chakra

From their Crown Chakra, bring the swirling bubble of golds and fireflies that is in your hands down to their 10th/ Earth Star Chakra, allowing time as the 10th fills with this energy.

Continue the spiral infusion up and around to their 8th/Gateway Chakra.

From the 8th, bring the swirling bubble of gold frequencies and fireflies that is in your hands up to the 9th/Soul Star Chakra.

Allow the swirling gold and firefly energy to expand into all levels of their field. Hold here as the client's energy field lights up with gold and the dancing firefly frequencies.

Step 5: Clear and Transmute Outer Gridwork

Move to the top of the treatment table. You will be working with the guides using a four-hooped filter provided by them. As they hand you a filter, start high above the client's head at the outer edges of their grids and fields. Assist the guides as you very slowly pull the four-hooped filter through the gridwork. The filters align and clear the Incarnation Grid, Soul Field Grid, Fascial Grid, and DNA Grid. Only one pass is needed.

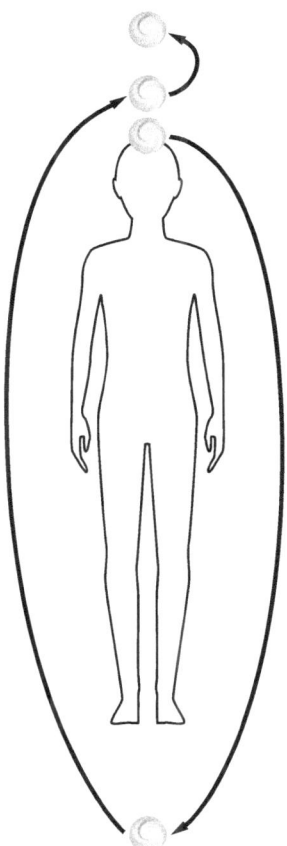

As you work with the four-hooped filter, invite clearing, alignment, and renewed purpose of this incarnation as the Incarnation Grid rewires. Ask the guides to help retrieve any aspects of the client's soul they may have given away. Then ask the client to release any aspect of the soul of others they might be holding for them. Invite all fascia restrictions to be unwound and reset for greater alignment. Ask that the DNA Grid open to transmute any misaligned genetics and any disruptive patterns in familial structures.

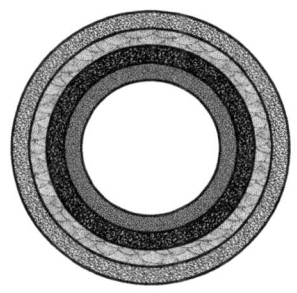

Step 6: Heart/Soul/Oversoul Connection
Come to the right side of the table, place one hand on the Heart Chakra and the other on the High Heart Portal at their Soul Seat. Invite the client's Oversoul to fully connect with their soul and their Heart Chakra. Allow balance and full integration as there is a weaving of these aspects.

- Heart Chakra: the will

- High Heart Portal/Soul Seat: the soul

- Oversoul: the highest frequency of soul

Hold here and just be witness and fully present to all aspects of the client's soul as the weaving and integration occurs. This may take a few minutes as full integration takes place.

Step 7: Primary Cell Unfurling and Infusion
Move your hands to a cupped position above the client's heart. Visualize your client's Primary Cell, wherever it might be in their body.

Invite their Primary Cell into your cupped hands. Hold their Primary Cell in sacred space. As you hold their Primary Cell, invite any bindings or restrictions to unfurl and to dissolve.

Continue to hold their Primary Cell as any bindings fully release and dissolve. Once the client's Primary Cell feels vibrant and full, ask their Core Essence to infuse the Primary Cell. Invite greater remembering of their soul's purpose in this incarnation.

Step 8: Remembering Divine Blueprint of Primary Cell
Holding your hands in this cupped position, bring their Primary Cell to the center line of their body. Slowly raise their vibrant Primary Cell through the body. From their Heart Chakra, move it up to the neck, through the head, and hold it just above the client's crown. Continue to slowly raise it as high as you can with your hands, then visualize as Primary Cell continues to travel up and connect with their Oversoul.

Hold in this spot, or you may bring your hands down to a more comfortable position with the intent that their Primary Cell stay at that high frequency connected with their Oversoul.

Invite a full remembering of the Divine blueprint of their Primary Cell at the Oversoul level. Hold space as this remembering occurs. Witness the vibrancy of Primary Cell as it expands and embodies that full potential.

Step 9: Recalibration of Lightbody to Primary Cell Potential
Continue to hold in this position and allow the Divine blueprint of Primary Cell potential to flow up into the client's Lightbody and matrix. Invite a recalibration of the Lightbody projection, fully aligned with the new potential of Primary Cell. When that feels complete, move your hands back down and hold just above the client's crown, inviting Primary Cell to hover just above the physical as the client integrates the Lightbody changes.

Step 10: Lightbody Activation Table
Standing along the right side of the table, ask that the treatment table be energetically transformed into a "light bright table," which appears as a crystalline structure under the client. Visualize the table becoming filled with glowing lights as the client gets infused with the perfect frequencies to activate the spin points and connection to the Lightbody. This prepares for the Lightbody recalibration and axiatonal alignment to facilitate the linking up of the Lightbody with the axiatonal grids, spin points, and multidimensional fascia.

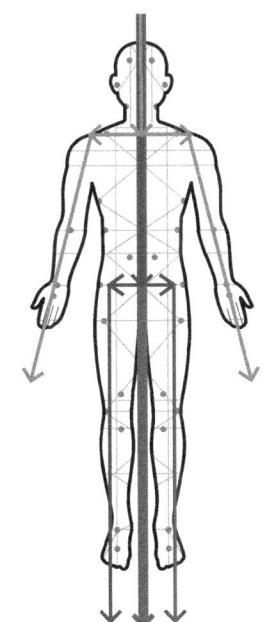

Step 11: Activation of Vertical Lines of Spin Points
Step toward the head of the table to trace the three lines of the spin points. Each set of three lines will be traced three times, as illustrated to the right. Reaching beyond the top of the client's head, draw your hands together, palms off the body, down through the center of the head. At the shoulder, split hands across each shoulder, tracing lines down each arm off the fingers. Again, reach your hands beyond the client's head to trace the second line. This line traces down through the center of the head and

torso. At the hips, your hands split to trace out across each hip, down the legs, and off the feet. Return to the top of the table to trace the third line. Again, begin tracing, hands together, from beyond the head, straight down through the head, torso, and straight between the legs, beyond the feet. Follow that pattern again two more times.

Step 12: Linking up Grids of Lightbody

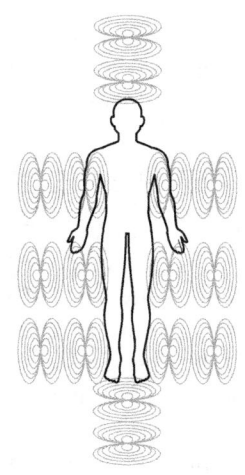

Move back to the top of the table, looking toward the client's feet. Linking up the grids will be accomplished with the help of guides duplicating your movements. The linking will be done in eight positions, three on each side of the body, plus one each at head and foot of the table. You will be leading the seven guides located at the other seven positions. Linking will be done by vertically tracing a double figure eight pattern, each loop of the pattern traces around the fields and grids. Hold the intent to weave through all the grids to each point (the intent to connect is what's important—not specifically physically connecting thousands of points). Guides facilitate through our etheric fingers to activate the spin points that weave interdimensionally.

Begin slowly drawing a double figure eight pattern down from above, crossing on the Incarnation Grid, crossing again in the Soul Field Grid, crossing next in the Fascia Grid, and lastly crossing in the DNA Grid, anchoring into the spin points in the body.

Repeat the tracing of the double figure eight pattern a total of three times as the group of seven additional guides simultaneously facilitate at the other locations around the client. See figure above.

Step 13: Activating Orion Helix

Continuing from the top of the table, trace the Orion helix (see figure next page) over the client's body. The pattern will be traced down three times and up, over the client's body. Draw the helix with both hands, palms off the body starting at 9th/Soul Star Chakra. Cross hands at: Brow Chakra, Heart Chakra, Solar Plexus Chakra, Navel/Sacral

Chakra, Root Chakra, knees, ankles, bottom of feet, 10th/Earth Star Chakra. Starting at Earth Star, trace the pattern in reverse up over the client's body. When reaching the Soul Star, repeat the pattern two more times down and up.

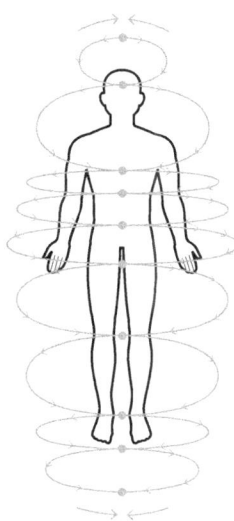

Step 14: Resetting Outer Gridwork

Move to the top of the table. You will be working with the guides using a four-hooped filter provided by them. Once they hand you a filter, start high above the client's head at the outer edges of client's grids and fields. This filter aligns the grid system with the transmuted Lightbody. It aligns the Incarnation Grid, Soul Field Grid, Fascial Grid, and DNA Grid. Assist the guides by very slowly pulling the four-hooped filter through the gridwork. Only one pass is needed.

Step 15: Integrations and Link-up of Primary Cell Frequency Through the Hara

From above the head, re-invite the client's Primary Cell back into your hands, then bring your hands along the Hara line. Allow their Primary Cell to slowly come down the Hara line through the lower seven Chakras and fields. Pause at each Chakra, allowing a short time for Primary Cell to link up with each Chakra and associated field (auric body).

- 7th/Ketheric Body
- 6th/Celestial Body
- 5th/Etheric Template
- 4th/Astral Body
- 3rd/Mental Body
- 2nd/Emotional Body
- 1st/Etheric Body

Finally, allow their Primary Cell to flow into the physical layers of the body. When this feels complete, bring your hands and Primary Cell to their heart, letting it rest there. Invite a full link up with every physical cell and their energetic matrix.

Step 16: Integrations Through Fascia and Lighting up of Biophotons

Moving up to the top of the table, reach out and cup the palms of your hands on each side of the client's head. Invite Primary Cell to connect and integrate through all of the fascia in their body. Set the intent to activate and illuminate the biophotons. Hold and witness as the biophotons light up and vitalize every cell as well as the entire body. This may take some time as each cell activates and becomes brilliant with the biophotons illuminating. Hold until there is a sense of completion.

Step 17: Anchoring Physically to the Pure Timeless Earth

Move to the bottom of the table and place the palms of your hands on the soles of the client's feet. Visualize a plasma with rich, iridescent neon orange energy pouring from the palms of your hands. Allow the energy of the iridescent neon orange to come up from the Pure Timeless Earth, grounding through the Vivaxis and anchoring Hara and flow through your hands.

Invite the iridescent neon orange frequency to flood up into every cell of the body, through bones, fascia, muscles, organs, and template of the body as well as all the fields. This will support these frequencies in grounding and anchoring to assist in strengthening the physical form.

Continuing to hold their feet, draw your awareness now to the client's 10th/Earth Star Chakra and connect it to the rich, iridescent neon orange energy.

Connect their 10th Chakra deeper into the core of the Pure Timeless Earth. Visualize the client connecting and weaving in with the multi-dimensional gridlines and matrices in the earth.

Hold and allow time for this to assimilate.

Step 18: Finalization

As a final step, the practitioner visualizes streamers of gossamer threads woven and infused with iridescent diamonds, swirling around and creating a three-inch-thick cocoon of energy encasing the client. This protects and holds the energy, allowing time to integrate and assimilate the gifts of the session.

Give gratitude to the many guides that have worked with you today.

Lastly, ground your client. Disconnect energetically and honor this beautiful Soul that you have had the privilege to work with.

Chapter Twenty

Your Soul's Knowing and Intuition

During the workshop, the evening time was purposely kept lighter and more playful, yet still providing opportunity for learning and personal insights.

We began the evening playtime with sacred sound and toning. We gave a brief overview of the concept of frequency with toning. The concept of resonance was discussed as every physical object has a vibratory frequency or resonance. If the toning is at the resonant frequency or a multiple of that frequency, transformative healing can be induced. We playfully experimented with vowel sounds and the scales to encourage use of voice and step beyond the inhibition many of us share about using our voice. Participants then explored and experimented with using their voices to find resonance and healing frequencies with a partner.

Then participants were organized in small groups for intuitive exercises. Participants brought the crystal that had been placed on their Heart Chakra earlier in the day for the Soul Embodiment Healing protocol. Each participant had a chance to tune into their crystal and intuitively seek guidance on the following questions as well as ask others in the group for their intuitive insights.

If you experimented with using a crystal while practicing the protocol, we encourage you to try this as well. If you did not use a crystal, try asking your subconscious for information. Read the following questions and ask for deeper understanding and clarity to flow forward for your highest good in this moment.

- Did you have any sensations or thoughts that came forward from the protocol (images, emotions, people, places)?
- Was there any resistance?
- Do you think your soul is trying to lead you somewhere?
- Do you have any desires that keep coming forward?
- Are others in the group getting information? If so, what might that be?

This exercise seemed to be well enjoyed by all.

The last "intuitive play" exercise was designed for the creative side of people. Participants were given paper, colored pencils, and crayons.

We had them ask the question: "What does your soul look like, feel like, or present to you?" Everyone who wished to draw was given sufficient time to create a drawing of their soul. Those who wished to share introduced their picture to the group and described what they sensed.

We encourage you to put down the book and do the "intuitive play" exercise. Invite your creative self to come forward. Pull out your journal or a piece of paper, colored pencils, pens, or crayons. Take a few deep breaths and drop into your Heart Chakra, asking from here what your soul looks like, feels like or presents as. Then, take some time to draw and see what comes forward! Share your picture with a friend or loved one if you like and describe what you sensed as you explored.

Chapter Twenty-one

Fascinating Fascia

We believe that fascia is a very important and poorly understood body system. Here we provide an overview of the fascial system to enhance understanding of the physical structure of fascia. This overview includes current perspective and understanding as well as some of the emerging views on the topic. We also bring forward our more multidimensional perspective of how the fascial system interfaces with the physical and energetic systems of the body.

Current Perspectives on Fascia

Every part of the body is wrapped in fascia. This multidimensional matrix creates the form and supports the function of every cell, organ, and tissue group, resulting in a 3D metabolic and mechanical matrix, which holds the shape of the body. Fascia communicates throughout the body via electrical signals, liquids, pressure, sound, and light.

Fascia develops from the "embryonic mesoderm into mature tissue,"[11] which becomes the musculoskeletal system, connective tissue, and organs. Fascia can vary in consistency. It can be a fluid substance such as blood or a solid such as bone. Between these two classifications is "supporting connective tissue," which is our most commonly understood definition of fascia.

---

11 Schultz, R. Louis, & Feitis, Rosemary. (1996). *The Endless Web: Fascial Anatomy and Physical Reality.* North Atlantic Books.

Three primary physical fascia components are:

- Cells
- Ground substance—gel-like "stuff" that acts as "filler," creating structure between organs, muscles, and other layers of tissue and as a transport system throughout the body
- Fibers—collagen, elastin and reticulin

These components combine to create at least 120 different types of fascia. It forms uninterrupted sheets from head to toe, from superficial layers under the skin to deeper layers connecting organs. Fascia weaves through and envelopes every cell, tissue, organ, and body structure such as blood, lymph, nerves, muscles, ligaments, tendons, and bones. Fascia forms thick bands that connect and support our skeletons. It applies tension and compression within the body's structures, which helps us hold our shape through a network of tissue. These systems of fascia work together in groups and communicate and interrelate. Our patterns of movement, posture, and injury compensation may become "programmed" into the fascia. Scar tissue or adhesions may bind and prevent free and fluid movement of limbs, spine, etc.

Bodyworkers such as massage therapists, structural integration practitioners, or physical therapists have developed multiple techniques to physically manipulate fascial tissue and break down dysfunctional tissue or movement patterns from injury or posture.

Emerging Perspectives on Fascia

Fascia plays a role in most of our body functions:

- Cellular respiration and elimination
- Fluid and lymph flow
- Metabolism
- Repair of tissues
- Conversion of body heat
- Fat storage
- Cellular health and immune functions

Fascia seems to define the shape and size of other tissue groups in the body. Any stretching and distortion of fascia can be felt throughout the entire system. Fascia may also be considered our second nervous system. It forms a communication matrix touching every cell. It appears that the meridians are embedded in fascial tissue and may be part of the fascia. The recently "discovered" organ called the interstitium, which is a fluid filled organ throughout the body, may also be part of the fascia system.

Many people now believe that fascia is a storage vessel for emotional energy. It can be manipulated physically and energetically to release stored trauma and emotions. Mental or emotional restrictions manifest as fascia restrictions and inhibit flow within the body's matrix.

The tissues of fascia are liquid crystal and conductors of electricity. Some of the tissues are like semiconductors and may act like little computer chips. Fascia tissue communication is by biophotons and micro currents.

Fascial Exploration Experiential

Taking a break from mental processing work, we invited the participants to explore the fascial system of their own body using guided imagery. We now invite you to go on an explorative journey with the fascia. Begin by relaxing wherever you are at this moment, get comfortable and centered, connected to Source, and ground in the Pure Timeless Earth. We invite you to place one hand on your thigh and attune with your body below the fabric of your clothing. Sense the top layer of your skin, the epidermis, noticing the frequency and characteristic of this tissue. Pause as you experience the sensations under your hand. Now, begin to sense a little deeper into the next layer of skin, the dermis. Notice whether you can sense a difference in the feel, structure, and frequency of this layer.

After a pause, we continue the journey inward, stopping at each layer to explore. Slowly travel down to the subcutaneous tissue, the fascial layers, the muscles, nerve bundles, periosteum tissue around the bones, the bone tissue, and into the marrow of the bone. At each layer give yourself enough time to sense and experience the frequencies, densities, flows of energy, and emotions through the tissues. When you feel like you have sensed all layers, slowly bring your awareness back up and out until you are sensing your hand on the fabric again. Take some time to journal your experiences.

Our Multidimensional Perspective

We think the energetic fascial system may be one of the least understood and most important systems in the body. Our physical body appears to develop along the grids or matrices of the 11th energetic level and the Fascial Field, according to and with the instructions provided at our 10th Chakra and DNA Grid. Our physical body organization, from cellular level to organ system, to our full human physical self is influenced by these unseen energetic aspects of self:

- Soul's purpose—8th/Gateway Chakra
- Our incarnation plans—9th/Soul Star Chakra
- Cell's DNA frequencies—10th/Earth Star Chakra
- Fascial Grid—11th/Connective Chakra and Tan Tien
- Golden structure of the 12th/Golden Matrix Chakra reshapes and purifies the distortions in our Being's perfect purpose

It appears that the meridians are embedded in the fascial tissue and may be part of the fascia. Fascial cells may form the tubules that created the meridians. The Nadis are an interdimensional distribution network. There are over 72,000 Nadis that connect the physical (fascia) with the energy bodies and grids. Nadis are like grid points (nodules) in the Fascial Field, embedded in and aligned with the field. Nadis are part of the web or network of the Lightbody matrix and Fascial Field. As Fascial Fields become distorted, the Nadi network and/or matrices of Lightbody can become distorted. In turn, any distortions in the Nadi network affect the Fascial Fields and matrices. Tissues or grids at all levels become compressed or feel out of alignment, causing issues in the physical body.

When we work quantumly, sound waves go out and through the Nadis in the physical and through all levels and dimensions of the fields and beyond. These waves interact with the Vibratory Grid (A "Sacred Sound Toning System") that exists in the dimension of sound. The Vibratory Grid is energetically parallel to the Nadis. We could think of them as the Nadis that are not physical but flowing within the energy system and beyond. The Vibratory Grid spin points correlate to acupuncture points, Nadis, meridians, fascial planes, and grids. The Vibratory Grid points are an interface with the meridians. This sound toning system is how the sacred ethereal sound of the Knights Paladin and Magenta Warriors affects the physical body. This system influences all aspects of us as it moves through the Grand Matrix.

We have noticed in some clients that interdimensional fascial parasites or nodules can be attached to fascia. These parasites can interfere with the heart-brain connection, limit the ability of the fascia to communicate, or even affect DNA and intercellular function. Fascia unwinding, releasing, repatterning, and realigning helps to flush them out.

Primary Cell can be instrumental in fascial healing. When an activated Primary Cell fuses with the heart fascia, it supports clearer embodiment of the fascia's Divine original blueprint, expands into all the physical fascia throughout the body, and realigns all grids and matrices. Fascia has its remembering of pure Divinity at a cellular level.

It is believed that the emission of biophotons and the production of sound by the fascia has a clinical significance, which at this time is still unknown. The vibratory and oscillatory patterns are present when they are recorded.

Working in the Fascial Field Grid

The Fascial Field can tear or have holes that affect function and healthy flow in the nonphysical as well as the physical body and fields. There can be scars, bindings, constrictions, etc. in the Fascial Fields that prevent healthy flow of energy, as a Chakra challenge inhibits or limits the physical structures relating to that Chakra. Healing energetic fascia assists the tissue—and ultimately the whole being—in remembering its original intent. It can reconnect us to our soul's purpose and ultimately to Source.

As a practitioner moves with intent through the Fascial Field, they may feel or sense a "ping" on their fingertips or different spots on the fingers when something is out of alignment. A "ping" or another sense of disruption occurs when a Nadi or another aspect of the Fascial Field is out of alignment. Misalignment of the Nadi's placement in the individual's matrix can become distorted when the Fascial Fields are distorted.

When working with restructuring and infusing the fascia, we can gently pull a Nadi back into an even better place in the matrix. Working with the Vibratory Grid and/or light matrix as the Knights Paladin and the Magenta Warriors are toning helps to restructure the Nadi networks and maintain the changes in the Fascial Fields after fascia work. Restructuring the fascia can help to realign other lifetime challenges. If someone has a "collapsed" auric field, you can intentionally find, expand, and work with the Fascial Field to restructure it. People with autoimmune issues often have compressed tissue (ex: fibromyalgia or chronic fatigue syndrome).

When working to bring balance and realignment to the fascia, we first sense into the Fascial Field and gridlines. We hold with a gentle tension at two locations or points between energy structures within the Fascial Field. Tight fascia can feel as though one is stretching a rubber band, either between layers or within a layer of the field. Follow the tissue as it unwinds through the Fascial Field. Allow the tissue to unwind at its own pace. It is a "following the energy" process. We are not directing, rather waiting, and following as the fascia leads. Be careful not to move too quickly and "snap it back" as it is restructuring.

When you feel or sense a "rubber band sensation," something is "amiss." (The feel is similar to when bodyworkers do a kind of myofascial release.) If we allow it, the tissue will unwind itself or slowly open and feel less taut. Gently hold until the tissue melts. It is inviting the remembering of the organizing matrix to know itself.

We utilize this understanding to guide our experiencing and healing of the multidimensional layers and structure of the fascia.

Fascia Unwinding, Releasing, Repatterning, and Realignment (Experiential)

Prior to teaching the full fascia protocol, we wanted to give participants a chance to experience and work with the subtleties of the fascial systems. For this exercise, participants were seated and standing. The receiver was seated, and the practitioner was either seated or standing as they needed to experience the exercise. We asked the participants to be curious and be the observer/explorer. There would be no need to figure out or judge or fix what they were sensing; the invitation was to just keep an explorer's mind.

We invite you to find a willing partner to explore the world of fascia. The person in a neutral role will be seated. The one in the sensing role will be standing.

We begin by asking the one in the sensing role to center and connect to Source and your Core Essence. Next, place one hand on the neutral person's thigh. Attuning into the physical layers, sensing into their tissue, sense the energy and note if it is smooth or perhaps has blocks, gaps, or congestion. Bring your other hand to the 5th layer/Etheric Template (blueprint of the physical body) of their field while still keeping the first hand on the upper leg. Again, note the difference in sensations, comparing the 5th level's field to the physical. (We invite you to trust yourself that you can sense the 5th layer of the field.)

Next, keep the one hand at the 5th layer and move the other hand to the 11th layer of the field. (Trust that you can sense the 11th layer.) Note the difference in sensations, comparing the layers. Sense any tightness, congestion, or blocks. If there are any distortions at the 11th level, can you discern if it feels like past life rather than a present life disruption?

Lastly, move one hand to the neutral person's Tan Tien at the lower abdomen, using the other hand to sense into the multidimensional Fascial Field. To some people, this field can feel more like the soul's intent, rather than physical structure.

Allow enough time to explore through the fields, experiencing the movement as the fascia released, unwound, re-patterned, or realigned.

As we sense in and move through the different layers to realign the Fascia Field, we are quantumly affecting the Fascial Field. This, in turn, quantumly affects the alignment of the physical fascia, 5th and 11th fields, and everything else.

When complete, switch roles and repeat the exercises. We encourage you to journal your experiences.

Multidimensional Fascial Unwinding and Repatterning Healing Protocol

Following the learning aspect for fascia, we demonstrated the protocol then proceeded to the experiential portion of the lesson. The experiential is done working in pairs at a treatment table. One participant takes on the role of practitioner, the other the role of client or recipient of the work. After the session is complete and time is taken for discussion and reflection, the participants reverse roles so that both have an opportunity to give and receive. If possible, we suggest that you find a partner to practice this experiential.

The purpose of this technique is to:

- Clear, unwind, and reset old fascial constrictions and blockages that are ready to release and allow freer movement in the physical body.
- Open pathways to release and shift old trauma patterns that might be held within the fascia.
- Support restructuring of physical and energetic fascia, the Nadi network(s), and matrices, as needed.
- Strengthen the bond of soul into the body for deeper embodiment of this incarnation.
- Rebalance, recalibrate, and realign Lightbody to be in alignment with client's soul's plan and the upgraded and balanced fascia system.
- Support healing on a cellular level through activation of the Axiatonal Grid system.
- Reweave the client's repatterned multidimensional fascia and energy system into the fabric of the earth grids, lifting the frequency of all humanity.

Step 1: High Frequency Shift: Self
The first step of the session is High Frequency Shift (HFS) for the practitioner. This is done while holding the feet of the client. The HFS brings the practitioner to the optimum elevated frequency to be the conduit for the client. It also serves to entrain the client in that elevated frequency, beginning the process of healing.

Step 2: High Frequency Shift: Client
The next step is to perform the client version of the HFS, ensuring the client is also at an elevated frequency.

Step 3: Charging Sequence
The Charging Sequence prepares the client for the deeper fascia work. This version of the Charging Sequence is highly supported by a group of guides as the practitioner uses their intent and visu-

alization skills to direct energetic frequencies through the client. We begin by standing at the foot of the table and consciously inviting Archangel Zadkiel to the head of the table and the 12 Indigo Masculine Knights Paladin to surround the client. Next invite the Divine Wisdom to the foot of the table. The 12 Magenta Feminine Warriors join in to create their ring of indigo/magenta around the client's energy field, encasing them in a bubble. As Zadkiel and the Knights Paladin are joined by Divine Wisdom and the Magenta Warriors, together they hold the outer edge of the client's field, as they tone their sacred ethereal sound. The 26 celestials will continue to encase the client and sound throughout the protocol to support loosening and unwinding of any fascial restrictions.

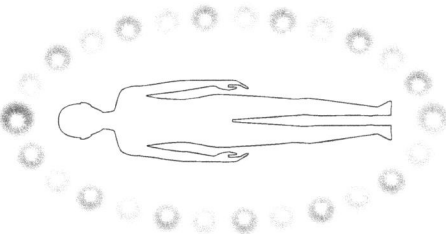

As the toning continues, place your hands on the bottom of the client's feet, one hand on each foot. At each position, the intent of the practitioner will be that the client's body open, cleanse, and charge with the frequencies invoked. As you hold the bottom of the feet, invite iridescent, effervescent chartreuse bubbles to flow up through the feet and lower legs with the intent of loosening and freeing trauma from the fascia in the body. Hold each hand position for at least a minute or longer, moving when that section of the body feels cleared and charged. Continue moving up the body with the flowing, iridescent, effervescent chartreuse bubbles loosening and freeing trauma from the fascia in the body. There are eight hand positions in the charging sequence as illustrated.

1. Hands on bottom of feet.
2. Both ankles.
3. Both knees.
4. Both hips.
5. Both wrists.
6. Both elbows.
7. Both shoulders.
8. Both sides of the head.

Step 4: Freeing Fascial Restrictions in the Body

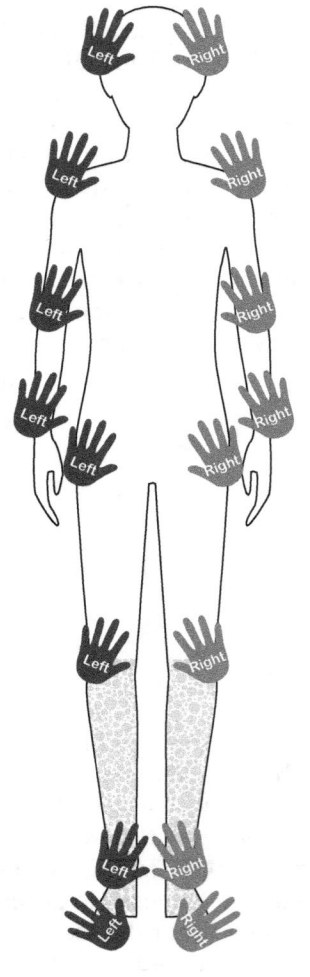

The Charging Sequence is completed with your hands on each side of the client's head. This next step starts with the same hand location. So shift your intent and awareness from charging frequencies and begin to bring your awareness into the fascial layers of the client's head. Start to sink into the fascia and invite releasing and unwinding of stuck fascial tissue. Invite the color frequencies of blue (cobalt, royal, and electric) along with gold. Sense as these frequencies flow through the client's head and neck. Continue to focus on the head and neck fascia, allowing the frequencies to loosen, release, and unwind all restrictions that are ready to realign. As this work proceeds, allow yourself to be guided and follow the energy as the fascia unwinds and restructures into new patterns that are more buoyant and freer within the head and neck.

When this feels complete in the whole head and neck area, move your hands to the client's shoulders. Continue to tune into the fascia now of the shoulders and upper body. As you sink into the fascia, invite a releasing and unwinding in these areas. Notice the color frequencies of blue (cobalt, royal, and electric) along with gold as they flow through the shoulders, arms, back, chest, and whole upper body.

When the loosening, releasing, and unwinding feels complete in this area, move to the right side of the treatment table along the side of the client. Place your hands at the client's 4th/Heart Chakra and 2nd/Sacral Chakra. Follow the fascia through the core muscles and lower torso. As you sink into the fascia, invite a releasing and unwinding of the fascial tissue here. Notice the color frequencies of blue (cobalt, royal, and electric) along with gold frequencies as they flow through the organs, to the psoas, and into the deep muscles of the inner body. There are many layers of fascia throughout the organs and other tissues. Be sure to allow time for the deep loosening, release, and unwinding of any constrictions throughout this area.

When this feels complete in the lower torso area, move your hands to the client's hips as you follow the fascia through the lower body. As you sink into the fascia, invite a loosening, releasing, and unwinding here. Bring the blue and gold frequencies into the whole pelvic area. Let the frequencies flow down the legs, through all the large muscles, into the ligaments, tendons, and intricate connective tissue.

When it feels complete in this area, move your hands to the client's feet as you follow the fascia through the lower body. Continue to invite releasing and unwinding of the whole physical form from the bottom of their feet to the top of their head. Hold until you sense a relaxation within all the tissues of their body.

Step 5: Energizing the Etheric Template
Move one hand to the client's thigh while the other hand connects with the 5th level of the field (Etheric Template). Here is the blueprint of the physical body. Continue to be aware of the toning of the celestial helpers as you sense the lines and movement of the 5th level. Notice the frequency difference between the physical body and the Etheric Template. Set your intent to energize the 5th level, allowing it to transform and transmute, preparing for the multidimensional work.

Step 6: Sensing the Fascial Field Grid
Move your hand that was on the thigh, placing that hand on the client's Tan Tien. Reach the other hand out to access the multidimensional Fascial Field. Begin to sense the difference connecting to the Fascial Field rather than at the 5th level. Hold here as you get a sense of the quantum connection between the Tan Tien and the Fascial Field. When you get a sense of that connection and tune in, release your hand from the client's Tan Tien.

Now, allow yourself to be led as the guides continue to tone into the Fascial Field. Sense the connections between the Fascial Field, 5th layer, and physical layer. Notice, sense, and use your hands to feel areas of constriction or density. Allow yourself to follow the connections, enabling them to unwind, release, and repattern. Slowly continue this work as you are led to unwind, hold, and follow any constrictions or obstructions within the Fascial Field. Notice as you slowly move along this grid that the client's body may shift on the treatment table as the rewiring occurs. Allow time for the releases and transformation. Continue to work moving into the multidimensional fields.

Step 7: Unwinding, Releasing, Repatterning, and Realigning Fascial Restrictions in the Multidimensional Field
Notice that as Zadkiel and the Knights Paladin as well as the Divine Wisdom and Magenta Warriors continue to sound, you continue to follow, release, and realign the Fascial Field, the 5th layer of the field, and the physical. You may get a sense or be guided to begin to use your own voice to tone into the fascia, trusting the sacred sounds that arise within you are perfect for the client. Follow your intuition with your toning. Notice when you feel thickness, compression, or density in the body or fields. This may be the place where your toning can support release and realignment.

As you feel the fascia shift, you may "follow" the tissue as it unwinds into the fields. You may feel a need to "stretch" or hold between two points or hold one and move your other hand along another line. You may simply hold as the tissue layers unwind themselves. Just trust and follow, even if it takes you under the treatment table.

Continue to follow. Allow your hands to sense and trace the patterns, releasing any blockages and supporting repair of any tears or distortions in the field. The guides are helping the client's tissues to unwind, dissolve old traumas, and repattern at the physical and into the fascial layers and fields. Pause where needed, then when an area feels complete, move on.

As the pattern returns to a more aligned—a more perfect reflection of its intent—you may also notice the Nadis brighten.

As the tissue repatterns or realigns, there are points at which you may adjust a Nadi or nudge it back into a clearer pattern. The entire field may then realign.

Let yourself be guided as you follow the energy to facilitate freeing any restrictions. Give yourself plenty of time and move slowly as the fascia shifts and realigns. It may take several minutes to complete.

Step 8: Additional Fascial Cleanse
Standing along the right side of the client, place both hands above their Tan Tien in the lower abdomen. Visualize and invite a rainbow titanium frequency to flow into the body's fascia through the Tan Tien, blending with the electric blue energy of fascia, flowing quantumly into all dimensions.

Allow this flow of rainbow titanium energy to clear old trauma stored in the physical fascia, 11th field, and all dimensions of self. This may take a few minutes. Hold until you get a sense of completion.

Step 9: Lightbody Activation and Recalibration
Standing along the right side of the table, ask that the treatment table be energetically transformed into a "light bright table." Visualize the table becoming filled with glowing lights, filling the client with the perfect frequencies to activate the spin points and connection to the Lightbody. This prepares for the Lightbody recalibration and axiatonal alignment to facilitate the linking up of the Lightbody with the extradimensional fascia.

Raising your hands, hold them with your palms facing the client's outer energy fields.

Invite recalibration and activation of the Lightbody to flow into the following gridworks creating new alignment:

- The client's matrix
- The Fascial Field Grid and the 11th layer
- The Incarnation Grid and 9th layer
- The Soul Field Grid and 8th layer
- The DNA Grid, quantumly resonating with the 10th Chakra

Next, place one hand on the client's Heart Chakra, the other on their High Heart Portal at their Soul Seat. Allow your breath to come into sync with the client's breath, inviting the recalibration of the holographic projection of Lightbody from all dimensions to flow down into all aspects of their being. Invite them to fully embody this new alignment. You will be assisted by guides as they do the work recalibrating. Just hold and be the space as you sense the shifts in the client's entire energetic structure. When this feels complete, move to the next step.

Step 10: Activation of Vertical Lines of Spin Points

Step toward the head of the table to trace the three lines of the spin points. Each set of three lines will be traced three times, as illustrated below. Reaching beyond the top of the client's head, draw your hands together, palms off the body, down through the center of the head. At the shoulder, split hands across each shoulder, tracing lines down each arm off the fingers. Again, reach your hands beyond the client's head to trace the second line. This line traces down through the center of the head and torso. At the hips, your hands split to trace out across each hip, down the legs, and off the feet. Return to the top of the table to trace the third line. Again, begin tracing, hands together, from beyond the head, straight down through the head, torso, and straight between the legs, beyond the feet. Follow that pattern again two more times.

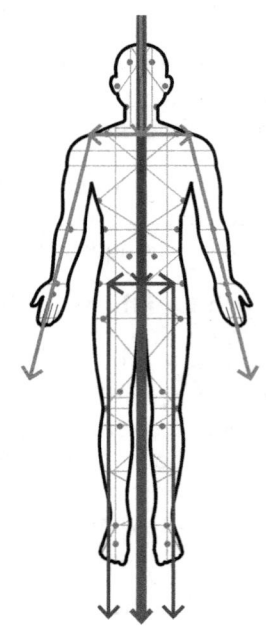

Step 11: Linking up Grids of Lightbody

Move back to the top of the table, looking toward the client's feet. Linking up the grids will be accomplished with the help of guides duplicating your movements. The linking will be done in eight positions, three on each side of the body, plus one each at head and foot of the table. You will be leading the seven guides located at the other seven positions. Linking will be done by vertically tracing a double figure eight pattern, each loop of the pattern trace around the fields and grids. Hold the intent to weave through all the grids to each point (the intent to connect is important—not specifically physically connecting thousands of points). Guides facilitate through our etheric fingers to activate the spin points that weave interdimensional.

Begin slowly drawing a double figure eight pattern down from above, crossing on the Incarnation Grid, crossing again in the Soul

Field Grid, cross next in the Fascia Grid, lastly cross in the DNA Grid, anchoring into the spin points in the body.

Repeat the tracing of the double figure eight pattern a total of three times as the group of seven additional guides simultaneously facilitate at the other locations around the client. See figure to the right.

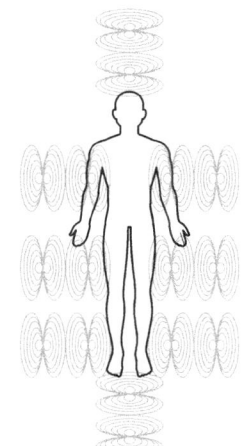

Step 12: Activating Orion Helix

Continuing from the top of the table, trace the Orion helix over the client's body. The pattern will be traced down three times and up, over the client's body. Draw the helix with both hands, palms off the body starting at 9th/Soul Star Chakra. Cross hands at: Brow Chakra, Heart Chakra, Solar Plexus Chakra, navel/Sacral Chakra, Root Chakra, knees, ankles, bottom of feet, 10th/Earth Star Chakra. Starting at Earth Star, trace the pattern in reverse up over the client's body. When reaching the Soul Star, repeat the pattern two more times down and up.

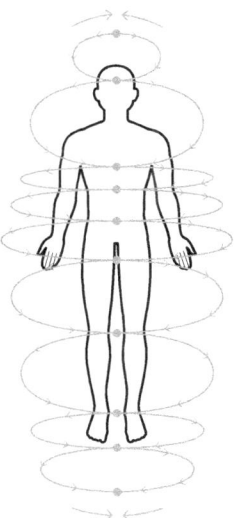

Step 13: Infusing Core Essence into Primary Cell

Move positions to be along the right side of the table. Hold your hands cupped above the client's heart. Visualize your client's Primary Cell and invite Primary Cell into your cupped hands. As you sacredly hold the Primary Cell, tune into the cell. You may get images of restrictions or sense binding on the cell, limiting its full potential. Invite in grace and let any bindings around Primary Cell dissolve; watch as it unfurls into its full vibrancy. Any bindings that might be holding your client back are released for full activation. As any bindings dissolve, invite your client's Core Essence to infuse their Primary Cell. Hold space and allow this infusion to flow as it may take a minute or more to come into full vibrancy.

Step 14: Primary Cell Infusion into Heart Fascia
Lower your cupped hands to the client's heart. Open your palms as you invite their Primary Cell to merge with their heart. Witness as the Primary Cell is infused into their heart. Using your breath to facilitate the movement, visualize breathing Primary Cell into the heart tissue, and expand the frequency of Primary Cell into all of the heart muscles and the heart fascia. With each breath, expand the client's heart fascia. Invite breaking of old restrictions to allow space for expansion and full expression. Notice as all the changes that occurred in releasing any trauma and emotions held in the client's heart and Fascial Fields dissolve. Allow this new genetic imprint from Primary Cell to infuse and imprint into the heart tissues. The guides will fill every cell of your client's heart with this upgraded Primary Cell genetic imprint.

With your breath, allow the new and revised frequencies to move beyond the client's heart.

Step 15: Expand, Release, and Entrain All Fascia
Continuing that expansion, use your breath and visualize the new genetic imprint and frequency of heart fascia spreading through the body, allowing every cell to be upgraded. Breathe it into:

- Upper chest
- Neck
- Head
- Back
- Right arm to fingers
- Left arm to fingers
- Torso
- Right leg to toes
- Left leg to toes

Feel the entire fascial system light up with new frequencies, free and elastic. Feel the client's whole physical body—expanded, vibrant, with a new genetic imprint. Allow their fascia to recalibrate as the whole energy system is synchronized.

Step 16: Re-Integrating Soul—Weaving with Möbius Coil
When all of the fascia has been infused with Primary Cell's new programming, re-weave the client's entire energy system to consolidate

and strengthen. Move to the side of the table, and using your hands, weave a möbius strip (a figure eight) from their 10th/Earth Star Chakra to 9th Soul Star Chakra, passing through the Heart Chakra to strengthen and consolidate the entire energy system. Trace this pattern with your hands several times until you sense the flow and movement becomes a möbius coil enveloping the entire energy system. Allow time as your weaving becomes consolidated, strengthened, and set. See figure below.

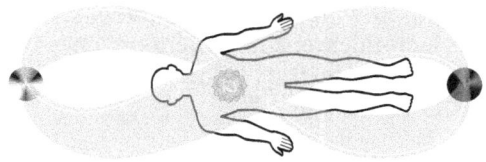

Step 17: Weaving the Earth Connections to Strengthen Embodiment
Move to the foot of the table. Hold the palms of your hands on the soles of the client's feet. Tune into the Pure Timeless Earth. Visualize connecting the client's 10th/Earth Star Chakra deep into the gridwork and matrices of the Pure Timeless Earth. Pause to allow full connection and linkup. You may sense them resonating with the frequencies of the core of the planet. When they feel in full resonance, visualize connecting their Earth Star with their Heart Chakra at the center of their chest. Allow time to fully connect. Then visualize connecting their Earth Star deeply into their individual Core Crystal deep within the earth. Allow the connection to be fully established, then connect their Core Crystal with the core of the Pure Timeless Earth.

Hold and invite a deeper integration. Witness as they become more embodied.

Step 18: Anchoring Physically to the Pure Timeless Earth
Continue holding the palms of your hands on the soles of the client's feet. Visualize a plasma with rich, iridescent neon orange energy pouring from the palms of your hands. Allow the energy of the iridescent neon orange to come up from the Pure Timeless Earth, grounding through the Vivaxis and anchoring their Hara and flowing through your hands.

Allow it to flood up into every cell of the body, through all the bones, fascia, muscles, organs, and template of the body, as well as all the fields. This will support these frequencies in grounding and anchoring to assist in strengthening the physical form.

Step 19: Finalization

Continue holding the client's feet as you ask Archangel Raphael to bring sparkling iridescent green light. It flows through your hands to flood the bones, fascia, muscles, organs, and template of the body, as well as all the fields to promote healing and finalization.

As a final step, the practitioner visualizes streamers of gossamer threads woven and infused with iridescent diamonds, swirling around and creating a three-inch-thick cocoon of energy encasing the client. This protects and holds the energy, allowing time to integrate and assimilate the gifts of the session.

Give gratitude to the many guides that have worked with you today.

Lastly, ground your client. Disconnect energetically and honor this beautiful soul that you have had the privilege to work with.

Chapter Twenty-two

Embodying Our Quantum Essence

This last protocol brings together the teachings from all segments of the workshop. The primary underlying focus of this workshop has been embodiment. All teachings have contributed towards encouraging and enabling deeper embodiment of our sacred self at all levels of our being. This expansive protocol opens us up to experience our entire quantum self. Inherent is the paradox of inviting the vastness of our true quantum self deeper into our awareness within the limited earthly conscious day-to-day existence.

The experiential is done working in pairs at a treatment table. One participant takes on the role of practitioner, the other the role of client or recipient of the work. After the session is complete and time is taken for discussion and reflection, the participants reverse roles so that both have an opportunity to give and receive. If possible, we suggest that you find a partner to practice this experiential.

The purpose of this technique is to:

- Create new extradimensional crystalline geometry through access of the Quantum Hara Points at higher frequencies conducive to greater embodiment.
- Clear the client's Hara, fields, and grids in preparation for deeper embodiment of our Soul and acceptance of our mission of this incarnation.
- Invite full embodiment of the client's soul DNA into their Primary Cell to encode the pure Divine template aligned with their soul's plan for this incarnation.

- Upgrade the client's Hara and Lightbody to new possibilities.
- Reweave the client's healed energy system into the fabric of the earth grids, lifting the frequency of all humanity.
- Heal, strengthen, and integrate all physical, emotional, mental, and spiritual aspects of the client.

Step 1: High Frequency Shift: Self
The first step of the session is High Frequency Shift (HFS) for the practitioner. This is done while holding the feet of the client. The HFS brings the practitioner to the optimum elevated frequency to be the conduit for the client. It also serves to entrain the client in that elevated frequency, beginning the process of healing.

Step 2: High Frequency Shift: Client
The next step is to perform the client version of the HFS, ensuring the client is also at an elevated frequency.

Step 3: Reconnecting to Pure Timeless Earth
It is important for this protocol that both the practitioner and client are deeply connected to the Pure Timeless Earth to ensure the purity of connections and access to the highest frequencies available.

Begin by moving to the foot of the treatment table, holding the feet of the client. Focus first on yourself and your full connection to Source. Then connect deep into the Pure Timeless Earth, connecting through your Core Crystal. Deeply tune into your Core Crystal. Allow your crystal to merge with the crystalline structure of earth as well as the matrix of the earth. Sensing into your Hara, run the frequency of Pure Timeless Earth from the core of the planet up through your Tan Tien, Soul Seat, and Point of Individuation. Feel your strong Hara.

Ask the guides to help bring the client's energy down into the core of the Pure Timeless Earth. Sense as their Core Crystal also merges with the matrix of the earth core. Let the client entrain with your high frequency.

Step 4: Extradimensional Charging Sequence
The Extradimensional Charging Sequence prepares the client for the deeper work of this protocol. The Extradimensional Charging

Sequence opens and balances the energetic body while raising the frequency of the entire field. This version focuses gridwork alignment into the newly activated Quantum Embodiment Points.

Note: The upper point of the triangles anchors into the Soul Embodiment Point between 8th and 9th Chakras. The lower point of the triangles anchors into the Incarnation Embodiment Point between the 10th Chakra and Core Crystal. This results in greater stabilization of the physical form to enhance the embodiment of our spiritual selves. The crystalline structure that's created supports the transmuting of non-beneficial energies and enhances the physical healing process.

This version of the Extradimensional Charging Sequence is highly supported by a group of guides as the practitioner uses their intent and visualization skills to direct energetic frequencies through the client. We begin by standing at the foot of the table and consciously invite Archangel Zadkiel to the head of the table and the 12 indigo masculine Knights Paladin to surround the client. Next invite the Divine Wisdom to the foot of the table with the 12 feminine Magenta Warriors to create their ring of magenta and are interspersed with the indigo around the client's energy field, encasing them in a bubble. As Zadkiel and the Knights Paladin are joined by Divine Wisdom and the Magenta Warriors, together they hold the outer edge of the client's field, as they tone their sacred ethereal sound. The 26 celestials will continue to encase the client and sound throughout the protocol to support loosening and unwinding any fascial restrictions.

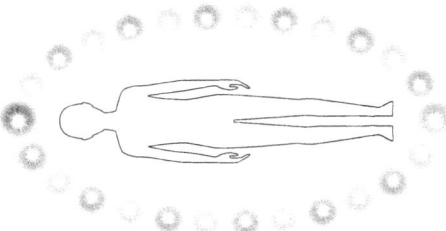

As the toning continues, place your hands on the bottom of the client's feet, one hand on each foot. At each position, the intent of the practitioner will be that the body open, cleanse, and charge with the frequencies invoked. The 26 celestials toning will clear and transmute in exactly the right way for this client in this moment.

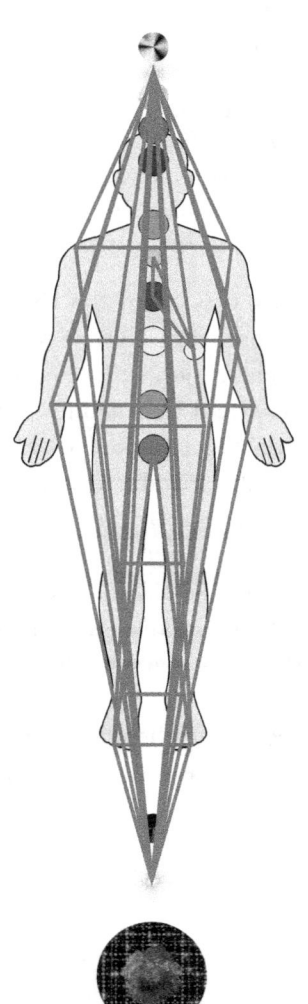

You will focus on the creation of the triangle and the energetic connections from your hands through all levels of the client's being. Hold each hand position for at least a minute or longer, moving when that section of the body feels cleared and charged.

There are ten hand positions in the Extradimensional Charging Sequence listed below and shown in the illustration to the right.

Charging Steps

The following are the hand positions.

- Solar plexus reflex points of feet—creating triangles to the Soul Embodiment Point and the Incarnation Embodiment Point.

- Same position, now connect to the Root Chakra and the Incarnation Embodiment Point.

- Both ankles—creating triangles to the Soul Embodiment Point and the Incarnation Embodiment Point.

- Both knees—creating triangles to the Soul Embodiment Point and the Incarnation Embodiment Point.

- Both hips—creating triangles to the Soul Embodiment Point and the Incarnation Embodiment Point.

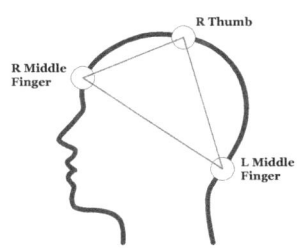

- Both wrists—creating triangles to the Soul Embodiment Point and the Incarnation Embodiment Point.

- Both elbows—creating triangles to the Soul Embodiment Point and the Incarnation Embodiment Point.

- Hands on the spleen and thymus, mentally connect to the Heart Chakra, creating a triangle of the three points.

- Both shoulders—creating triangles to the Soul Embodiment Point and the Incarnation Embodiment Point.

Position right middle finger on the Brow Chakra, position left middle finger on the Zeal Chakra (at center indent point on occipital ridge). Position both thumbs on the Crown Chakra. Visualize a triangle connecting these three points, activating the head centers. See illustration top of page.

Step 5: Weaving the Quantum Hara
Step to the right side of the table. Bring your focus into the client's Hara. See illustration to the right.

Begin by visualizing a möbius strip connecting the client's Core Crystal and 10th/Earth Star Chakra.

Focus on the point where the möbius strip crosses. This is the Incarnation Embodiment Point. Let that point activate and expand its energy.

When that point feels activated, shift focus to the High Heart Portal and Heart Chakra, visualizing a möbius strip connecting those two centers.

Focus on the point where the möbius strip crosses. This is the Soul Access Point. Let that point activate and expand its energy.

When that point feels activated, shift focus to the 8th/Gateway Chakra and 9th/Soul Star Chakra, visualizing a möbius strip connecting those two Chakras.

Focus on the point where the möbius strip crosses. This is the Soul Embodiment Point. Let that point activate and expand its energy.

When that point feels activated, shift focus to the 9th Chakra and Oversoul, visualizing a möbius strip connecting those two centers.

Focus on the point where the möbius strip crosses. This is the Oversoul Access Point. Let that point activate and expand its energy.

Now that these four points are activated, weave a möbius strip through these Quantum Hara Points, connecting them and weaving them together as shown in the figure.

This activates the notes within Hara, creating an opening in Soul Seat.

Invite widening of the client's Hara to accommodate the greater energy of this expansion and activation.

Step 6: Clearing the Hara
Stand at the right of the client's treatment table. Invite the guides to clear the client's activated Hara. The guides will be doing this work. You may witness or assist as they reach into the base of the client's Hara at their Core Crystal with their long etheric fingers. The guides will use color and frequency to clear, transmute, and purify the Hara. They slowly raise their fingers, combing through the Hara from base to top. You may sense things being removed and cleared as the work progresses. The guides will make three passes from bottom to top. Each pass uses the perfect color and frequency to purify.

When the guides complete the clearing, they will infuse the Hara with chartreuse frequency from the core of the Pure Timeless Earth, through the client's Core Crystal, and up through the entire Hara. It may seem to come in like flames of chartreuse as it fills and infuses the chartreuse frequency to amplify the strength of the Hara.

Step 7: Quantum Expansion
Step to the foot of the table. Move your awareness and hands to below the client's feet, visualizing that you connect to the client's 10th/Earth Star Chakra. Invite the Pure Timeless Earth energy to flow up and meet iridescent earth tones to fill their Earth Star Chakra. Invite the iridescent earth tones deep into the zero point of the 10th. At the zero point where there is both nothing and everything, imagine a swirling galaxy of energy. Let the frequencies of iridescent earth tones flood into the 10th. Invite the swirling galaxy to open, infuse, and expand iridescent frequencies. The frequencies flow and spread waves of quantum energy as they expand out, filling the 10th level of the field. Invite the client's Core Essence to infuse the 10th level. Infuse the galaxy and field with the frequencies of the trinity gold, the white-gold, rose-gold, and pure-gold. Invite this galaxy and quantum waves to expand into the client's DNA Grid, the matrix, and all the organizing principles and instructions for their body. Invite the client to sense and experience this infusion and expansion.

Move along the right side of the table and hold your hands above the client's 1st/Root Chakra.

Visualize Pure Timeless Earth energy from the core flowing up into their Root Chakra as a vibrant, iridescent red. Allow the energy to penetrate deep into the zero point of root, seeing an iridescent galaxy at the zero point of root. Allow the galaxy to expand, sending quantum waves out to their 1st layer/etheric body. Invite their Core Essence into the etheric layer, filling the etheric layer with Core Essence. Invite the white-gold frequency into the gridwork of the 1st/etheric layer and fuse it with their Core Essence.

Shift your awareness and your hands to the client's 2nd/Sacral Chakra, inviting the Pure Timeless Earth energy in as iridescent orange to their Sacral Chakra. Visualize the orange going deep into the zero point, becoming an iridescent orange galaxy. Sense the vastness fill and expand the sacral as that galaxy expands, becoming quantum waves flowing out into their emotional body. Invite their Core Essence into the 2nd layer/emotional body. Invite the client to sense the flow and fluidity within the emotional body as it fills with Core Essence. Feel the waves and blending of Core Essence with rose-gold and all the beautiful colors of emotion.

Shift your awareness and your hands to the client's 3rd/Solar Plexus Chakra, inviting the Pure Timeless Earth energy in as iridescent yellow to their Solar Plexus Chakra. Invite that iridescent yellow deep into the core of the zero point of the solar plexus. As their Solar Plexus Chakra flows and expands, it becomes a galaxy of beautiful iridescent yellow. Let it shine brighter and brighter, expanding and flowing quantum waves into the gridwork of the 3rd layer/mental body. Invite their Core Essence to light up the grid-work of the mental body. Invite the frequency of white-gold into the 3rd layer, blending it with Core Essence. Invite the client to experience the blending of white-gold and Core Essence as the mental body gridwork stabilizes and renews.

Shift your awareness and your hands to the client's 4th/Heart Chakra, inviting the Pure Timeless Earth energy as iridescent green to their Heart Chakra. Invite the iridescent emerald green deep into the zero point as it becomes an expanding galaxy of iridescent green. Let that galaxy get bigger and bigger, expanding out through their chest. As the galaxy expands it sends quantum waves out into the 4th layer/astral body. Invite their Core Essence out into the astral body, filling that fluidic layer with their light. Invite the rose-gold frequency to infuse and blend with the movement and colors of the 4th layer. Invite them to sense and "be" with their Core Essence and feel the flood of colors and movement of the healing frequencies.

Shift your awareness and your hands to the client's 5th/Throat Chakra, inviting the Pure Timeless Earth energy in as iridescent sky blue to their Throat Chakra. Invite the iridescent sky blue deep into zero point of throat, flowing, expanding, and becoming a glowing blue galaxy of light. Feel the awe as the expanding galaxy floods quantum waves out into the lines and grids of the 5th layer/etheric template, lighting it up. Invite the brilliance of their Core Essence into the gridwork of their etheric template. Invite in the frequency of white-gold, fusing with Core Essence, flowing through all connections in that gridwork. Ask the guides to optimally align the gridwork of the etheric template to greater support the physical form. Allow time for the gridwork to stabilize, inviting the client to experience this layer.

Shift your awareness and your hands to the client's 6th/Brow Chakra, invite the Pure Timeless Earth energy in as iridescent indigo to their brow. Invite the iridescent indigo to flow deep into the zero point of the Brow Chakra, flowing and expanding into a galaxy of indigo light. As the galaxy expands it flows quantum waves out into their 6th layer/celestial body. Invite their Core Essence to fill and illuminate the celestial layer. Invite rose-gold to infuse and blend with Core Essence, brightening the celestial body. Invite the client to sense the joyful iridescent colors of that layer, perhaps hear the angels singing, feeling the peacefulness of this beautiful celestial layer.

Shift your awareness and hands to the client's 7th/Crown Chakra, inviting the Pure Timeless Earth energy in as iridescent violet to their Crown. Invite the iridescent violet deep into the zero point of Crown Chakra, flowing, expanding, and becoming an iridescent violet galaxy. Allow the galaxy to beautifully expand and flow, deepening the connections with the Divine. As the galaxy expands it showers quantum waves out to their 7th layer/ketheric template, the golden egg. Invite their Core Essence into the gridwork of the ketheric template, blending with the light of Source. Invite in the frequency of white-gold to join in an intense light in the ketheric template. Invite them to "be" and experience this layer.

Shift your awareness and your hands to the client's 8th/Gateway Chakra, inviting the Pure Timeless Earth energy in as iridescent silver to their Gateway Chakra. Invite the iridescent silver deep into the zero point of 8th, flowing, expanding, and becoming a galaxy of iridescent silver. As the galaxy expands it sends quantum waves into the 8th layer, vitalizing and brightening the layer. Invite the clients Core Essence into the 8th layer. Invite in the frequencies of the trinity gold—white-gold, rose-gold, and pure-gold—to expand out into the 8th and quantum connections into the Soul Field Grid.

Invite the client to tune in to the 8th level of their field, sensing the blending of these beautiful energies.

Shift your awareness and hands to the client's 9th/Soul Star Chakra, inviting the Pure Timeless Earth energy in as iridescent copper to their Soul Star Chakra. Invite the iridescent copper deep into the zero point of the 9th, flowing and expanding, becoming a galaxy of copper. Let the expanding galaxy flow quantum waves of copper out into the 9th layer. Invite their Core Essence to infuse the 9th layer. Invite in the frequencies of the trinity gold—white-gold, rose-gold, and the pure-gold—to imbue the 9th layer with these energies. Invite the client to sense the brilliance of the 9th level of their field and the quantum connections into the Incarnation Grid. Invite their Core Essence into that grid, aligning them with the matrix of this incarnation.

Moving to the right side of the table, expand your arms and bring your awareness to the client's 11th/Connective Chakra. Invite the Pure Timeless Earth energy in as iridescent metallic blue to their 11th. Invite the metallic iridescent blue of the Connective Chakra into the client's hands, feet, Nadis, and all around them as they become surrounded by a large metallic blue galaxy. Feel this galaxy of the beautiful metallic blue color, move your awareness into this galaxy, and expand with the galaxy. Invite their Core Essence to fill and brighten the galaxy. Invite in the frequencies of the trinity gold—white-gold, rose-gold, and the pure-gold—to imbue the galaxy. As the galaxy expands it sends out quantum waves into the 11th level of the field and quantum connections of the Fascial Grid. Allow time for the quantum waves to integrate and stabilize the Fascial Grid. Invite the client to sense into the Fascial Grid, touching every aspect of their Being.

Continue standing on their right side. Shift your awareness to the 12th/Golden Matrix Chakra. Invite the Pure Timeless Earth energy in as iridescent gold into their Golden Matrix Chakra. Invite the iridescent gold into the zero point of the 12th Chakra creating a brilliant iridescent golden galaxy around them. Invite their Core Essence and the trinity gold to infuse the swirling galaxy. Allow the swirling galaxy to expand and flow quantum waves into their entire Lightbody. Invite the client to fully inhabit their Lightbody and to let their Core Essence BE that vibrant iridescent gold. Know that this is who they truly are!

Give gratitude to the multidimensional being they are and the opportunity to share this expansion.

Step 8: Bringing Soul DNA into the Physical DNA
Continue standing on their right side and use your hands to trace a möbius strip. Create the möbius strip between the 9th/Soul Star Chakra and 10th/Earth Star Chakra. Begin at their Soul Star, cross at the Heart Chakra, and weave down around Earth Star. Weave the Soul DNA from 9th Chakra into a physical DNA imprint held in the 10th Chakra. Weave several times as you invite the client's Soul DNA to blend and imprint into the physical DNA at the 10th Chakra. Continue the flow until it feels set and complete.

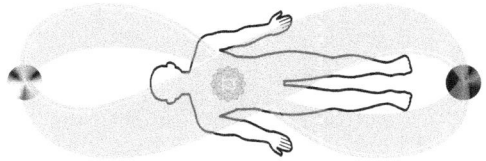

Step 9: Bringing Soul DNA into Primary Cell
Next, hold your hands open, palms up above the client's heart. Invite their Primary Cell into your hands. As you hold, BE the sacred space for full activation of their Primary Cell. Invite in grace and let any bindings around Primary Cell dissolve; watch as it unfurls into its full vibrancy.

Invite the full embodiment of their Soul DNA into their Primary Cell. Hold until the Primary Cell feels flowing, full, and vibrant.

Step 10: Primary Cell Infusion into Heart Fascia
Lower your cupped hands to the client's heart. Open your palms as you invite their Primary Cell to merge with the heart and fuse the new genetic imprint into the heart. Visualize the link up of energy between Core Essence, Heart, and Oversoul.

Using your breath to facilitate the movement, visualize breathing Primary Cell into the heart tissue, and expand the frequency of Primary Cell into all of the heart muscles and the heart fascia. With each breath, expand client's heart fascia, breaking old restrictions to allow space for expansion and full expression of all the changes that occurred in releasing any trauma and emotions held in the client's heart and Fascial Fields. Allow this new genetic imprint from Primary Cell to infuse and imprint into the heart tissues. The guides will fill every cell of your client's heart with this upgraded Primary Cell genetic imprint.

With your breath, allow the new and revised frequencies to move beyond the client's heart.

Step 11: Expand, Release, and Entrain all Fascia
Continuing that expansion, using breath, visualize the new genetic imprint and frequency of heart fascia spreading through the body, allowing every cell to be upgraded.

Breathe it into:

- Upper chest
- Neck
- Head
- Back
- Right arm to fingers
- Left arm to fingers
- Torso
- Right leg to toes
- Left leg to toes

Feel the entire fascial system light up with new frequencies, free and elastic. Feel the client's whole physical body—expanded, vibrant, with a new genetic imprint. Allow their fascia to recalibrate as the whole energy system is synchronized.

Step 12: Bringing Full Embodiment into the Multidimensional Self
Move to the end of the table and hold the client's feet. Bring your

awareness to the full embodiment of all aspects of your client's Being. Invite this embodiment to move beyond the physical into all dimensions, as you quantumly connect the levels of the fields with the upper grids of the client. Pause and be present as you witness this full embodiment flowing into all aspects and weaving throughout each layer of their multidimensional self. Sense as the client becomes full and vibrant, aligned and connected to all aspects of self.

- 8th /Soul Field Grid
- 9th /Incarnation grid
- 10th /DNA Grids
- 11th /Fascial Grid
- 12th /Physical and all layers
- Tan Tien/Hara

Step 13: Remapping the Lightbody to the Upgraded Hara
Move up to the top of the table. You will be working with the guides to remap the client's Lightbody. The guides will give you filters to recalibrate and integrate their Lightbody. Start high above the client's head, at the outer edges of their grids and fields, asking that their Lightbody be recalibrated and integrated with the upgraded Hara. Imagine holding a large hoop as the filter. Slowly pull the filter down the table, remapping as you go with the filters provided by the guides, integrating the Lightbody from top to bottom. After the first pass, return to the top of the table as the guides give you another filter. It typically takes three passes to complete the remapping. Stay at the bottom of the table after the third and final pass.

Step 14: Infusing Pearlescent Frequency Through the System
Stand at the foot of the table and hold the bottom of the client's feet. Visualize the client's Core Crystal within the earth. Invite the color and frequency of pearlescence into their Core Crystal, infusing it with the pearlescent frequency. When their Core Crystal is fully infused, bring your awareness to their Hara, beginning to infuse the Hara with the pearlescent frequency and color. As you continue to hold their feet, slowly invite the pearlescence color and frequency to rise up the Hara,

coating the inside and outside of their Hara. Allow the pearlescence to begin soothing, stabilizing, and flowing into all dimensions of their Being as it calms and supports the new Hara structure. Continue to invite a flow of the pearlescence up their entire Hara all the way to Oversoul.

Step 15: Illuminate the Fireflies

Continue to hold the client's feet. Shift your focus into the client's physical layers. Invite their biophotons to light up. Witness the client becoming a brilliant, luminescent Being. Invite the luminescence to expand. Sense and experience how the client is connected with all humanity.

As the frequencies meld, there is an igniting and activation with all the gridlines of the earth to invite full embodiment of what this client's soul's purpose is, as their true purpose weaves with the Pure Timeless Earth. Hold here as you sense awe and wonder within the client as they fully embody their soul and their purpose.

Step 16: Align and Entrain the Frequencies of the Universe and Divine Matrix

Staying at the client's feet, sense out to the unimaginable distances of the universe and multiverse. Give gratitude for all of creation. Invite the Universal Masters and all benevolent universal beings to assist and give grace. Invite the client to align with all pure matrices. Attune and align with the frequencies of the Divine Matrix of all creation and the collective woven into the matrix.

Step 17: Let the Energy Flow Through Into the Earth

Reposition your hands to hold your palms on the soles of the client's feet. Go into surrender mode. Sense and allow every aspect of you to know this state of being. Be aware of the frequency that flows through the client now, know it as love. Invite these frequencies to flow into the earth, raising the frequency of earth and all beings on the planet.

Feel the immense gratitude from beings at all levels being thankful for this gift. Reflect back to them gratitude and love.

Step 18: Zipping Up the Field

Zipping up the field helps the client integrate the very expansive frequencies they have been receiving and brings them back to a more normal level of energetic expression. Begin by holding the bottoms of both feet. You will be holding a pattern of hand placements for about 10 seconds or so in each position, connecting the left and right sides of the physical body. Follow the sequence as noted and shown in the figure.

The finishing position holds hands on both sides of the head.

- Holding the palms of your hands on the soles of the feet.
- Left ankle and right knee.
- Right ankle and left knee.
- Left knee and right hip.
- Right knee and left hip.
- Both hips.
- Left wrist and right elbow.
- Right wrist and left elbow.
- Left elbow and right shoulder.
- Right elbow and left shoulder.
- Both shoulders.
- Left shoulder and right side of head.
- Right shoulder and left side of head.
- Both sides of the head.

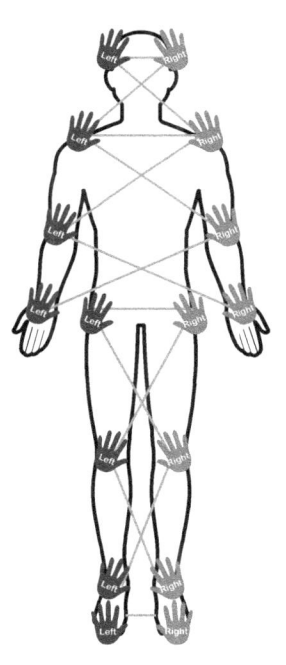

Step 19: Finalization

As a final step, the practitioner visualizes streamers of gossamer threads woven and infused with iridescent diamonds, swirling around and creating a three-inch-thick cocoon of energy encasing the client. This protects and holds the energy, allowing time to integrate and assimilate the gifts of the session.

Give gratitude to the many guides that have worked with us today.

Lastly, ground your client. Disconnect energetically and honor this beautiful soul that you have had the privilege to work with.

Chapter Twenty-three

Holding the Frequency

On the last morning of the workshop, we reviewed its major themes and discussed how to hold the frequency. Past workshop participants have noted two issues that arise following our multi-day events. One issue is reentry, and the other long-term maintenance of the frequencies. Our work intent creates an elevated frequency that is amplified by the group process. Existing in this elevated state for multiple days allows the energy to build and go to higher frequency levels than most people can achieve in their daily lives.

The first concern—reentry into the world of everyday life—is a temporary situation, but it helps if one knows the potential exists and to just be aware and stay present. Some who have attended previous workshops made plans to immerse themselves back more slowly into daily life to make the transition smoother.

The second long-term concern is what we spend more time discussing. We provide tools to help individuals maintain higher frequency in daily life. However, most of us need encouragement to make the small changes to daily practice, seek connections with others, and ask for help when we need it.

We hope that by reading this book you have been able to tap into the higher frequency work and have achieved some of the benefits enjoyed by those that attend a live event. Even though you are not in the same room as the group that is also reading this book, you are connected to the other readers and joined with them in ways that you may never know. Therefore, the question applies to you as well:

How do you retain the highest possible frequency in everyday life when faced with the myriad of daily distractions?

You Are Light!
How Do You Keep Remembering This Every Day?

High Frequency Shift is part of the secret. Practice daily or at least multiple times a week. Make note to practice it more often during especially stressful times!

- Connect to Source.

- Connect deep into the Pure Timeless Earth.

- Strengthen and align the Hara.

- Focus on flow in each Chakra.

- Expand and raise Core Essence.

- Invite connection to all of humanity and allow the universal energies of love to flow through you.

Achieving this goal is usually not instantaneous. Step by step, we deepen the embodiment. Day by day, we spend just a little more time in that state. Trust that we will go up and down with our frequency. Life is like a roller coaster. Going up and down is just part of the journey, it doesn't mean we have failed or are less on the days that we don't do as well.

Mind your thoughts! Remember that you create your own reality. What you think shifts your energy expression. Your energy expression shapes your attention, which shapes your perception of the world. That perception registers as your experience, reinforcing your thoughts and beliefs. You will see the world exactly as your thoughts predict, just as if held before a mirror. If you want to change the world, it is only a thought away.

Self-love takes daily practice. Make peace with your past and learn to love yourself first. Practice daily these qualities of love until you can honestly say that you treat yourself as good or better than you treat your best friend:

- Compassion
- Acceptance
- Generosity
- Gratitude
- Grace
- Respect
- Honor
- Empathy
- Understanding
- Forgiveness

Try self-intimacy ("into me I see") occasionally in a mirror. Can you see your Core Essence, that beautiful Divine Being that you truly are? Look for and acknowledge that inner light in others as well.

Affirmations are a wonderful way to practice until we can believe in ourselves. Practice reclaiming your sense of self as pure love by using this affirmation sequence:

- I am my Core Essence, in oneness with Divinity.
- I am in alignment with my Oversoul, supporting me to be love.
- I allow my Soul to shine through me and guide me as love.
- I know that my earthly appearance is an aspect of love.
- I forgive and accept my human form and limitations, knowing I am love.
- I fill myself with grace to act in love.
- I fill myself with generosity to self and others.
- I lower my walls of protection to accept love.
- I am love and I am being love.

Practice self-awareness and self-referencing. Stop periodically to bring a focused attention to your own energy system. Practice this until it becomes a natural part of your observation of the world. Notice those things that make you brighter and more expansive. Be aware of the things that bring you inward or make you smaller. Notice who is helpful and who you find more challenging to hold your energy strong in the presence of. When you notice, experiment to see how you can change those energetic interactions. Practice generosity, grace, gratitude, awe, and wonder, and notice how they affect your energy.

Practice awareness of others and other-referencing. Every interaction with another human is energetic. Notice your two-way interactions with those close to you as well as the strangers you pass by in the grocery store or public places. Practice this until that awareness becomes part of your normal attention range. Experiment with an understanding of how you hold your energy. When in higher frequency, does the interaction change? Is it more graceful? Play with it so you can hold your energy strong and stay in integrity.

Practice deep presence and continued embodiment through all 12 Chakras. Periodically come back to this list and focus on the role that each of your Chakras play in maintaining deep presence and strengthening your embodiment:

> **1st/Root Chakra:** Who you are in the present moment as you allow for greater embodiment.
>
> **2nd/Sacral Chakra:** Dissolve all unhealthy cords, keeping only the loving heart connected cords.
>
> **3rd/Solar Plexus Chakra:** Full balance in your sense of self and all your human relationships.
>
> **4th/Heart Chakra:** Honor yourself as worthy of love, made of love, capable of fully loving, and accepting love in this embodied form.
>
> **5th/Throat Chakra:** Embrace your soul's Divine journey on earth.
>
> **6th/Brow Chakra:** Trust Divine guidance and your soul's plan.
>
> **7th/Crown Chakra:** Believe that any experience in your life is perfect and in Divine order.
>
> **8th/Gateway Chakra:** Feel your connection with Oversoul and see your soul's roadmap.

9th/Soul Star Chakra: Recognize that you ARE a spark of the Divine! This is a window to your own pure Soul, your Core Essence at its highest frequency.

10th/Earth Star Chakra: Embody and have the willingness to accept the lineage you came onto the planet to support.

11th/Connective Chakra: Be aware of and ask for a weaving and strengthening, connecting into all the matrices and gridwork of the Pure Timeless Earth.

12th/Golden Matrix: Allow for integration and full embodiment of YOU as the Divine Being of Light, here and now, as you are held by the shell around all the energy fields.

Maintain activation of your Quantum Hara Points. Add this awareness into your daily self-care routines. When focusing on the Hara, consciously focus on maintaining activation of the Oversoul Access Point, Soul Embodiment Point, Soul Access Point, and Incarnation Embodiment Point. As you focus on these points, invite deeper embodiment of your Divine self. Ask your soul to come deeper and embrace a deeper listening. Keep remembering that you are your soul, and you have a plan. Events happen for you, not to you. This grand plan of the soul is all encoded in your Lightbody.

Keep exploring the fascinating world of fascia. Find a partner to work with sensing and exploring fascia and the amazing information it holds. Explore the physical layers of fascia as well as the 5th and 11th layers of your field. And most importantly, the Fascial Field, which is the multidimensional framework of the fascia matrix.

Dance with the fireflies! Find the awe and wonder that abounds in our world. Light up your bioluminescence. Remember that you are part of the web of light that interconnects all humanity.

YOU ARE ONE OF THE LUMINARIES!
LET YOUR LIGHT SHINE!

Chapter Twenty-four

Closing Invocation: April 2023

We finish the workshop in ceremony, using the following invocation to reinforce the learning and help set the new frequencies as the participants return to their everyday lives. The closing ceremony also included a ritual to cement their bond as a group and commit to global service. The same space was used for the opening and closing circle ceremonies. The group slowly spoke the closing invocation two times. The closing invocation was an affirmation of the transitions and personal growth the participants had experienced in the previous days. This ceremony used the stepping on the Merkaba symbol as they left the circle, as a symbol of completion. The phrase they recited leaving the circle was: "I step out of this time and space as a luminary."

We invite you to use the following as a meditation for anchoring the experiences you have had and embodied within the writings of this book.

Divine Delight: Embodying Your Soul

I stand in the template of the Pure Timeless Earth, my awareness fused with the crystalline matrix of our planet.

I inhale deeply connected into the powerful energy of earth, my entire being activated.

I bow in honor to the ancestors, elementals, and benevolent beings embodying and protecting this and all space. I am grateful for the ease and safety I experience.

My inner awareness holds a deeper remembrance and presence
in my being. I feel the pure love that is my sacred self.

I open my arms and embrace the Divine light of Source.
The luminescent fireflies fill me. Source radiates from me.

I breathe in, experiencing the new Divine frequencies
of pure love. I am a vessel of unified awareness;
I am the embodiment of sacred self.

I have released all limited ideas of self and reality.
I embrace all quantum shifts within my being
as I embody my soul on this lifetime's journey.

I commit to clear personal boundaries and
compassionate energetic interactions with others.

I am a servant of the Divine plan, embracing the highest
possible frequencies and dimensions flowing through me.
These frequencies purify and amplify all aspects of my
being, accelerating self and planetary ascension.

I am filled with gratitude and awe, my soul aware
of its luminous place in the fabric of creation.

My heart rejoices in the union of the masculine and
feminine aspects of the Christ Consciousness
and to my Oversoul. I am awake!

I open my arms to embrace the Divine light of Source.
I am filled, one with Source.

Chapter Twenty-five

Creating Our Body of Work

In 2015, the triad of co-creators began meeting regularly via phone. This evolved to video conferencing twice a month, and by late 2016, we decided to create a collective work to bring forward to the public in order to share our guided joint information. In the fall of 2017, we hosted our first retreat together in Colorado Springs, Colorado.

We continued to collaborate as a collective, bringing the work forward with new material for each retreat. In time we added additional collaborators. This guided collaborative process and series of workshops has spawned a considerable collection of works.

Some of AHA's work has already been brought forward in other workshops or in print with our published books: *The NEW Chakra Playbook [2024], I am Sensitive and Smart [2024], Soy sensible e inteligente [2024], Revealing Higher Frequencies [2024], Embodying Higher Frequencies [2022], Awakening to Higher Frequencies [2021],* and *Everything is Energy (including you!)[2020],* which was recently translated into Spanish: *Todo es energía (¡incluso tú!)[2025].* As we progress in sharing our work, we intend for it to be the subject of additional books and/or web-based material, focusing on and embracing the following topics and concepts:

- Limitlessness of Your Soul
- Enhancing Your Ability to Guide Self & Others From the Heart
- Nurture Your Intuitive Gifts
- Evolving Your Human Energy System to Meet the More Advanced Souls Arriving on the Planet

- Learn New Ways of Sensing into the Physical Body and Expand Your Skills to Assess, Access and Heal
- Exploring the Energetic Interaction of the Mycelial Network and Human Consciousness
- Deepening Self-love as a Physical Manifestation

Chapter Twenty-six

Conclusion: Final Notes

It is our wish that the work that we have shared supports the evolution of humankind by contributing to the collective of Lightworkers on planet earth and connecting to the vast consciousness of Light Beings that are ever present for us to raise all souls to even higher frequencies.

We know that this work is one of many paths that the supporting guides use to bring in the new frequencies to the earth in support of our common evolution. We hope that each of these paths merge into a clear road for humankind to find its way home.

We realize that we are but a small group that holds this high frequency of light for the collective, but we fully trust that we each make a difference in this evolution. Our intent is to build on our expanding web-based content to support the material in this book. Our hope is that expanding access and enabling all types of learners to study the material will lead to broader sharing of the highest possible frequencies.

Tim and Franny

Appendix

Glossary

Advanced High Frequency Shift (AHFS): An updated and more detailed exercise to train your energy system to access more of the highest available frequencies and prepare for the more advanced energies as our evolution continues.

Angels: Spiritual beings that act as messengers or agents of the Divine. Available to assist us when asked. It is thought we are always surrounded by angels, and each of us has one or more guardian angels.

Ascended Master: A spiritual being that was once in human form, mastered ascension, and karmically not required to incarnate. Part of the team of spiritual beings assisting humanity to evolve and ascend.

Ascension: The process of ascending to a higher spiritual level, level of enlightenment, or higher state of consciousness.

Axiatonal Grid: Axia=axis or direction; Tonal=sound or vibration; Electrical in nature, the Axiatonal Grid combines color and sound to realign blood, lymph, and the nervous system into Divine template. The Axiatonal meridian system is part of the step-down process from Lightbody to physical body. Equivalent of acupuncture meridians but connecting the Oversoul and resonant star systems with the physical. Through the Axiatonal lines, the gridwork of Lightbody is translated into programming of the human body.

Basic High Frequency Shift (BHFS): Exercise is foundational to training your energy system to access available frequencies and prepare for the more advanced energies now coming through.

Consciousness: The awareness of self and one's surroundings.

Core Essence: Your Light, the Divine spark of God that you are now, have been, and always will be. The position of Core Essence is the current expression of the frequency you are in this physical dimension. It also embodies the frequencies that reflect or represent other aspects of you.

Empath: A highly sensitive person with an ability to sense, experience, or take on the thoughts, feelings, emotions, or physical pain of those around them. Many empaths experience these sensations yet have trouble discerning the origin of the sensation.

Energetic Inserts: Energetic inserts are subtle programs inserted into our matrix or body. Think of them as like an app on your phone or computer. They can change our energy, behavior, and even our physical structure. They can be beneficial or non-beneficial. Obviously, we want to keep the beneficial ones and eliminate the non-beneficial ones. It is best to use the wisdom of the guides when transmuting inserts.

Energy Therapy: A therapy (there are many versions) where a trained practitioner consciously works with the human energy field and energy matrix of a client to restore balance and harmony.

Etheric Fingers: An energy (or energy lines) that extends beyond our physical fingertip. This is part of our etheric body or energy field (aura). We can use our visualization skills to stretch our etheric body beyond the physical body, in this case stretching our etheric layer as fingers. We work with etheric fingers to clear and move congested energy from the energy fields.

Extradimensional: Originating and operating outside the known physical three-dimensional physical reality. Working in many dimensions beyond the normal 3D of time and space.

Flower of Life: Sacred geometry form, at least 6,000 years old. Contains fundamental forms of time and space. We use it as protection and as a vehicle.

Frequency: In electromagnetics, it refers to the numbers of waves that pass a fixed place in a given amount of time. So it is basically the rate of vibration.

Guardians: Spiritual beings that serve a role as protector, sentinel, or defender.

Guides: Our team of Spirits (usually disincarnate) that serve to teach, guide, and protect us.

Hara: Column of energy we incarnate on. Our intents of life purpose creates an energetic connection from Spirit to form on this planet. Hara has an internal structure and an external structure.

High Frequency: Heightened levels of energetic awareness and existence. When in a state of high frequency, the human energy system functions at a more optimum state and has greater awareness of higher levels of consciousness.

Holograph: In our 3D world, a Hologram is a projection of a light field as an interference pattern that creates a light field. That field produces an accurate reproduction of the original image such that it can be viewed from different angles and creates the illusion of a true 3D object. Our usage of the term is from the perspective of a multidimensional reality where projections into the Matrix from many dimensions creates holographic fields which carry organizing energies and can be perceived by some sensitive people.

Ketheric: The seventh level or layer that is a structured, spiritual template of the energy field. The seventh Chakra is the doorway to this seventh level of the energy field that resonates with Divine Oneness.

Lightbody: A holographic projection upon the Matrix comprising many organizing fields. These fields define our spiritual and physical manifestation in this world.

Merkaba: Considered to be a Lightbody vehicle used to connect with and reach higher frequencies. It also is known to be multidimensional, allowing access to the other planes. It is used as a tool by Archangel Metatron.

Metatron's Cube: A representation of how energy flows through the Universe. It contains all Platonic Solids also holding 13 circles within. It is used as a cleansing device.

Möbius Strip: A möbius strip is a continuous surface with a twist in it. A simple example can be made by attaching the ends of a ribbon to each other with a single twist. We commonly use one that looks like a figure eight. Additional twists can be added to create more complex objects. Wires wrapped in a möbius strip can create scalar waves.

Möbius Coil: A möbius coil is a series of möbius strips that can create a continuous surface with a twist in it. Our physical structure has examples of möbius coils in our DNA at a cellular level and vascular system on a larger scale. These biological structures create scalar waves, thought to be part of the intercellular communication system.

Orion Helix: A helical pattern (multiple interlinked figure eights) that is traced up and down the body through the spin points as part of the healing techniques presented by AHA, including the Vibratory Grid Activation as taught in Hovland's work.

Oversoul: The primordial or highest level of soul, where it retains both the properties of being the self as well as being the selfless one. Oversoul resonates with the highest frequency of your soul in this plane.

Quantum: Properly defined as the smallest unit of many forms of energy. At the smallest of scales of quantum physics, the rules of interaction become different from classic physics. Our use of the term refers to complex interdimensional interactions of energy at this smallest scale.

Quantum Hara Points: Points in the Hara that allow for deeper embodiment of our sacred selves. These points are not new or "discovered," they are points that have been dormant in recent times. The energy of the planet and human evolution has moved to a point where these points are now accessible to be activated.

Rays or Ray of Light: A title for a specific or focused consciousness of the Creator. In this usage, light is information. Each Ray is already part of our soul waiting to emerge. The Rays are a form of teaching this information—they are a Discipline or Study of Divine Light.

Tree of Life: The tree of life is a geometric pattern or symbol used in multiple mystical traditions, generally associated with the Kabbalah. Although there are many interpretations, it usually depicts the process of moving the primordial energy of Source into the physical manifestation of this creation. In the reverse direction it could symbolize the spiritual ascension of humanity.

Vibration: An oscillation or movement of a fluid, elastic solid, or medium, or an electromagnetic wave.

Vibratory Grid: A "Sacred Sound Toning System," existing in the dimension of sound.

Vivaxis ("Axis of Life"): Your own personal generator in the energy field into which you are born. Formed within a few weeks of your birth. An agreement between the Earth and the Soul that will support what you came here to do in this lifetime.

Zeal Chakra: This Chakra is located at the base of the skull at the center of the occipital ridge. Supports accessing, gaining, and speaking higher wisdom and knowledge. We use the Zeal Chakra in bringing balance to a specific triangle and activation in the brain.

Bibliography

Bailey, Alice. *Esoteric Healing.* Lucis Publishing Company, 1953.

Baumann, S., Joines, W. T., & Kruth, J. G. Electromagnetic emissions from humans during focused intent. *Journal of Parapsychology*, 76, 275-294, 2012.

Bioluminescence. (2025, March 13). In *Wikipedia*. https://en.wikipedia.org/wiki/Bioluminescence

Brennan, Barbara Ann. *Light Emerging: The Journey of Personal Healing.* Bantam Books, 1993.

Dale, Cyndi. *The Subtle Body: An Encyclopedia of Your Energetic Anatomy.* Sounds True Adult, 2009.

Dale, Cyndi. *The Complete Book of Chakra Healing* (2nd ed.). Llewellyn Publications, 2010.

Emmons, Robert A. *The Little Book of Gratitude: Create a Life of Happiness and Wellbeing by Giving Thanks.* Gaia Books, 2016.

Glasson, Natalie. *The Twelve Rays of Light.* Derwen Publishing, 2010.

Hovland, S. "Vibratory Grid Activation." Unpublished notebook, 2000.

Jacka, Judy. *The Vivaxis Connection: Healing Through Earth Energies.* Hampton Roads Publishing, 2000.

Kessler, Steven. *The 5 Personality Patterns.* Bodhi Tree Press, 2016.

McCraty, Rollin. *Science of the Heart Volume 2: Exploring the Role of the Heart in Human Performance.* HeartMath, 2015.

McFetridge, Grant. *Peak States of Consciousness: Theory and Application*. Institute for the Study of Peak States Press, 2004.

Neff, Kristin D. The development and validation of a scale to measure self-compassion. *Self and Identity*, 2, 223-250, 2003.

Nienaber, Jeannette. *The Heart in You: A Personal Journey through Your Physical, Emotional, Mental and Spiritual Heart*. Balboa Press, 2019.

Noël, Rudy. *The Huggin' Healer*. Publish America, 2011.

Oxford University Press. (n.d.) Empathy. In *Oxford English Dictionary*. Retrieved January 31, 2025, from www.oed.com/search/dictionary/?-scope=Entries&q=empathy.

Oxford University Press. Gratitude. In *Oxford English Dictionary*. Retrieved January 31, 2025, from www.oed.com/search/dictionary/?-scope=Entries&q=gratitude.

Oxford University Press. (n.d.). Wonder. In *Oxford English Dictionary*. Retrieved March 28, 2025, from https://www.oed.com/dictionary/wonder_v?tab=factsheet#14252761.

Schultz, R. Louis, & Feitis, Rosemary. *The Endless Web: Fascial Anatomy and Physical Reality*. North Atlantic Books, 1996.

Sheldrake, Rupert. (2009). *Morphic Resonance: The Nature of Formative Causation*. Park Street Press, 2009.

Srinivasan, T. M. Biophotons as subtle energy carriers. *International Journal of Yoga*, 10(2), 57-58.

About the Authors

In order to understand our collective, it may help to see where we each came from and how those individual stories join to create the work that is Awakening Healing Axis. We believe that all are on their own path in just the right place. For those reading, it is no accident that you are doing what you are doing and at some level ready for the mystery of what this work may bring to you. The following is each of our stories leading up to the creation of our workshops. [Note: There is a language shift in the following stories from "I" to "we" as each author describes their individual experience.]

After working together for several years, Tim McConville and Franny Harcey were divinely guided to share their collective wisdom, and Awakening Healing Axis was born. Through the synergy of their collaboration, they have found it possible to go much deeper into the work of personal healing and supporting others in their quest for self-healing and transformation. With individual backgrounds in various energy modalities, Tim and Franny have created work that focuses on raising their collective frequency and those they share with, in order to contribute to the ascension of human consciousness.

This unique approach incorporates new healing techniques, increasing our understanding of the science supporting energy therapies while linking to the development of new insights among esoteric healing, human physiology, and energy therapy through the multi-dimensional bio fields. To learn more, please visit awakeninghealingaxis.com.

Franny's Story

Growing up in Minnesota, my perfect day was being outside communing with nature. I also found great solace in going to church and connecting with God in the way I knew at that time. When I was really young, I saw myself being a nun one day. Later, I shifted to following my heart and connecting with the Divine through meditation and a deeper personal spiritual connection.

As a small child, I was quite aware of "seeing and sensing" the spirits around my parents' home. I remember them vividly, but when I reached the age of about seven or eight, they began to frighten me for some reason, so I adamantly tuned them out and shut off my ability to see and sense them. I don't recall my abilities returning until I was in my late 20s when I had my children.

My early career was as a hairstylist. Working on clients' hair and being in such close proximity to them was a difficult time for me, as I am strongly empathic and had little ability to discern what was mine and what was not at that time. I would experience physical sensations such as pain or emotional upset, including tears. I recall thinking I was a bit loopy and going crazy. In truth, I was in serious energetic overload.

In 2000, I was pointed to a Healing Touch class. The energy training was lifesaving as I finally began to realize my empathic nature and gifts. It took me a long time to discern what was mine and what was not and how to self-regulate and support my own energy instead of unconsciously taking on someone else's challenges.

Over the course of more than two decades, I have studied with great healers and feel very blessed to have been present with so many at the time that I was so that I could embrace many different ways of being, learning, and bringing forth healing work. Each added to my toolkit to support me in the continual opening to the gifts I have and why I am here on the earth at this time. Since then, I have had the honor of working with thousands of clients over the past 20 years.

One of my great passions is mentoring others in the healing arts. I am blessed to be able to mentor many energy workers that are exploring who they are and how to be the best that they can be, first for themselves and then for the family, friends, or clients they work with.

Tim's Story

I have spent much of my life as a seeker. I was raised Catholic, but by adolescence, I yearned for more than Catholic teachings were offering. During much of my adult life, I voraciously read about all things metaphysical. At some point, I realized that what I was looking for could not be found in a book. I also participated in meditation groups and dabbled in some healing work. I made a few spiritual trips to India, spending my time in ashrams and studying Vedic spirituality. I considered myself a closet mystic, as most of my time went to career and family. I didn't really dive deep into healing work until my 50th year.

My college training was in environmental engineering. Much of my career focused on applying computers and automation to environmental issues. As a manager and VP in a consulting engineering firm, I was reluctant to share my deeper interests publicly. My work world was full of scientific thinkers who tended to be skeptical about things that could not be measured. I, too, struggled internally as my engineering training taught me to trust the scientific process. It took a couple of firsthand experiences to convince my engineer brain that the energetic world is truly real.

For the last 20 years, my interests and priorities shifted to the healing arts and exploring the unseen world of the spiritual. I was formally trained in Healing Touch and then expanded into other modalities. 15 years ago, I retired early from the corporate world to devote my efforts to teaching and client work in the energy healing field. As my healing and teaching practice grew, so did my trust in the unseen guides that would show me different techniques to use for healing.

Our current work is built on that deep trust and the ever-expanding possibilities that unfold as we deepen our understanding of our spiritual and energetic nature.

Apprentices and Contributors

We would like to honor the contributions of the apprentices that contributed to the making of these workshops. They have said yes to working with Spirit and assisting the entire collective to raise its frequency.

Barbara DeMers

Barbara owns and operates a hair salon where she offers integrative energy healing services in addition to her spirit-filled presence behind the salon chair. Barbara empowers her clients to realize their Divinity through aligning their energy system, allowing the innate shift for healing to occur. Her passion is creating an energetic environment for harmony and balance, thereupon revealing the Truth of who we are. She has studied many healing modalities and is an ordained minister. Barbara has been expanding with Awakening Healing Axis since the first retreat and eagerly stepped into the role of AHA facilitator.

Sylvie Francoeur

Sylvie is a proud Healing Touch Certified Practitioner and has been trained in several other healing modalities. She is also an instructor of the HT for Children program. Sylvie is a certified trainer with the Canadian Mental Health Commission and has over 25 years' experience as a facilitator, helping organizations navigate change. She has deepened her personal spiritual journey since connecting with Awakening Healing Axis in 2018. She is thrilled by the love and light being brought forward by the AHA team and is humbled to be able to share this work, as a contributor, with an ever-growing number of people.

Perry Harcey

As a child, Perry was sensitive to universal energies and had an innate knowing of information. He would use his hands and focused thoughts to heal his own physical wounds. Being mechanically inclined and process oriented, Perry used his gifts in an aviation maintenance career as a technician, inspector, and manager. Many times, Perry found himself using his energetic awareness to connect with the aircraft and receive information on what it needed, which helped to trouble-shoot, repair, and maintain the aircraft.

Within Awakening Healing Axis, Perry applies his gifts and knowledge to provide business and technical support services. He supports the energetic structure of AHA and receives and shares guided information for the support of the AHA community. With excitement and gratitude, he holds an integral part of AHA. Perry is committed to assist in bringing forward this body of work to support energetic and physical healing and to support the ascension of the collective human consciousness.

Joanne Kaufman

Joanne has been a Nationally Certified Massage Therapist since 2001 with an Associates in Occupational Studies (AOS) from Boulder College of Massage Therapy. She has studied, practiced, and received life-changing energy medicine work in numerous modalities. She integrates other energetic modalities and AHA's powerful energetic foundations and techniques into her massage therapy work. Joanne spent formative years in her 20s doing faith-based nonviolence work in conflict zones. In this work, she noticed how simple presence and deep listening allowed local partners to create new possibilities in their personal and communities' lives. This foundation underlies her particular passion for empowering each person to own, embrace, and follow their own healing paths and talents in their own timing. This commitment to deep listening to support each being's song has surfaced an affinity with crystals, as well as participating in the healing of Earth/Gaia. Joanne is so delighted and honored to be an AHA facilitator.

Jon Skedsvold

It was during Jon's deployments to Iraq (2003) and Kosovo (2009) that he started becoming keenly aware of the abundance of human suffering. This created in him the yearning to ask the deeper questions in life. "Who am I?" and "Why am I here?" The curiosity he had as a child came flowing forward as he began to contemplate these questions. As it turns out, asking those questions led him on an inner quest that he could not have imagined. Reading any book and talking to any person that seemed to lead him closer to the answers, he soon realized that the answers could only come from within! True knowing would come with personal deep healing. Delving into various healing modalities from others to support his personal healing proved invaluable. In 2019 Jon began studying Healing Touch, completing the first 3 Levels of Healing Touch Program curriculum. In October of 2020 he attended his first Awakening Healing Axis workshop. AHA created a deeper level of healing through these retreats and the incredible frequencies being introduced. It is with great excitement that Jon brings the wisdom he is guided to bring forward and to be a part of the AHA team and community. "I am humbled to have an opportunity to support this incredible work in the world."

Other Work by Awakening Healing Axis

Everything is Energy (including you!)

Awakening to Higher Frequencies:
A Guidebook

Embodying Higher Frequencies:
A Guidebook to Accelerating Personal and Planetary Consciousness

Revealing Higher Frequencies
A Guidebook to Exploring Personal Growth and Self-Love Through
Deep Reflection Using the Divinity Mirror and Energetic Expressions

I am Sensitive & Smart
Exploring Energy with Younger Empaths

Soy sensible e inteligente

Todo es energía (¡incluso tú!)

Work Co-Authored with Catherine Morgan

The NEW Chakra Playbook
Fun, Easy, Powerful Ways to Lift Your Chakras to the Next Level

———

AHA offers web-based training to deepen the experience of the energies described in this book. These are useful tools for both those who are interested in self-development as well as the practicing energy practitioner. Our experience suggests that more frequent practice helps to entrain your energetic system to the higher frequencies, allowing one to experience these elevated states for longer and more frequently, thereby changing your experience in the world. Links to all AHA trainings are available on our website.

To learn more about AHA's work, including upcoming books, workshops, and retreats, please visit:

www.AwakeningHealingAxis.com